FORT CLINCH, FERNANDINA
AND THE
CIVIL WAR

FORT CLINCH, FERNANDINA
AND THE
CIVIL WAR

FRANK A. OFELDT III

THE
History
PRESS

Published by The History Press
Charleston, SC
www.historypress.com

Front Cover
Top: A newspaper artist's drawing of the interior of Fort Clinch just days after being captured by federal forces. *Courtesy of the State Archives of Florida.*
Bottom: Companies C and E, First New York Volunteer Engineers carried out the construction of Fort Clinch. *Courtesy of the State Archives of Florida.*

Back Cover
The United States Colored Troops took an active part in serving at Fort Clinch and Fernandina during the Civil War. *Courtesy of the Library of Congress.*

First published 2020

ISBN 9781540243881

Library of Congress Control Number: 2020938459

*To my wife, Samantha, for her support and encouragement
and for the many times my love of history came first.
And to Mom and Dad, who gave me a compass to follow.*

CONTENTS

ACKNOWLEDGEMENTS

I would like to thank the many friends and associates who offered their help to bring this book into production. I want to thank the State of Florida's Archives for the many times they provided me with the documents I needed to fill in the gaps. I also need to thank the Library of Congress, the National Archives and their outstanding institutions for providing me with a wonderful opportunity to view the many papers, articles and documents related to the Civil War. I would like to extend my thanks to the Center for Military History, the United States Army Corps of Engineers and the United States Military Academy for the information they provided. Professor Penny Sansbury deserves my thanks for her knowledge of writing and literature, which led her to assist with the manuscript editing. I would also like to thank her husband, Steve Sansbury, for being an outstanding friend and fellow Civil War historian and for his free counseling on matters of great importance. I want to thank my coworker and close friend Andrew Smith for his input and knowledge of political science and how Civil War politics played out. I also want to thank Jennifer England for her help with images and her grandfather Howard England for taking the time to share his passion and love of Fort Taylor, where my career with the Florida Park Service started. My friend Mary Agnes White, who provided me with many letters and images of Fort Clinch before her passing, also deserves my thanks. I would also like to thank my friend and author Lewis G. Schmidt for all the documents he provided over the years. I thank Dicky Ferry for the wonderful original letters, documents and images he provided. Lastly, I would like to thank the Amelia Island Museum of History for the wonderful historic collection it preserves and the many living historians who volunteer to keep history alive at Fort Clinch and who recognize the role it played during the Civil War.

INTRODUCTION

F lorida's role in the American Civil War was small compared to other southern states. The state population was a mere 140,424, according to the 1860 census, with 61,745 classified as slaves. The largest towns were Marianna, Apalachicola, Pensacola and Quincy, followed by Tallahassee, Monticello, Madison, Fernandina, Ocala, Gainesville, St. Augustine and Key West. After becoming the twenty-seventh state to join the Union on March 3, 1845, the state played a major role in the Civil War as the chief provider of beef cattle and salt for the Confederacy. Florida was known as the "smallest tadpole in the dirty pool of secession." Although Florida was not a large cotton producer like its neighbors, it still produced the crop in the region that ran from Ocala in north central Florida to Marianna in the northwest. Floridians at the time had a strong stance on the issue of states' rights. With disputes over economics, political differences and slavery, the steam over the issue was building up, and the top was about to blow off.

With the election of Abraham Lincoln as the sixteenth president of the United States, Florida's path was clearly shown. Most Floridians supported southern democrat John C. Breckenridge, who received a vote of 8,543, and Unionist candidate John Bell received 5,437 votes. Fernandina's voting male population strongly supported the southern Democrat and the course of action of secession that was about to play out. The Civil War would become the greatest conflict the nation would endure during the nineteenth century. Even to this day, over 150 years later, Americans still debate the causes of the war and attempt to understand it.

One thing about the war that stands out for most is the loss of life that occurred. The Civil War's casualties were horrific, with almost one million dead and many others who suffered from long-lasting physical and psychological effects. The war affected just about every American, from those in the largest cities to those in the smallest towns, and its impact can still be felt today—even on Amelia Island, a place of sun and fun, where "island time" is the motto. The remains of the war can be seen in the places that the citizens of Fernandina called home so many years ago. Amelia island is the northernmost barrier island on Florida's east coast and has been a place that has seen great strife and sacrifice from its citizens since the first Europeans arrived there.

In 1811, the town of Fernandina, which is located on Amelia Island, was plotted by the Spanish during their second period in Florida, from 1783 to 1821. Today, there are two towns located on Amelia Island, both New and Old Fernandina. Old Town was founded in 1811, and New Town was founded in 1853 and remains today. The histories of these towns are unique; Fernandina was once a thriving seaport that boosted commerce trade, smuggling, slavery and profiteering. The town was named for King Ferdinand VII in 1811; at the time, he was prisoner of the French, but after the defeat of Napoleon, he regained the Spanish throne in 1814. Old Fernandina was a gem of a town, with grid-pattern streets and a location overlooking the Amelia River. The river was the town's lifeline to the world, where the ships brought forth the goods for the survival of citizens and the town itself.

Being a gem comes with envy, and in 1807, the United States instituted an embargo on all foreign goods entering the country. And a year later, in 1808, the importation of slaves to America was banned. Fernandina became a hot spot for smugglers, slavery and piracy until the embargo was lifted. Anything a heart desired could be found in Spanish Fernandina. In 1812, the Patriots overthrew the Spanish and captured the town; however, their occupation was short lived, and American forces took custody of Fernandina until the Spanish authority could be reestablished.

In June 1817, the Scottish mercenary Sir Gregor McGregor seized Fernandina and Fort San Carlos from the Spanish and raised the green cross flag of the Republic of Florida, liberating the island and its citizens from Spanish rule. However, with dwindling forces and finances, McGregor was forced to give up his conquest. Two Americans working alongside him seized leadership of the remaining forces and intended to maintain independence from Spain. Ruggles Hubbard, a former sheriff of New York, and Jared Irwin, a former congressman of Pennsylvania. The Spanish began to bombard Fernandina and Fort San Carlos, which were held by Irwin, Hubbard and their Republic of Florida forces of only about ninety men. The Spanish gunboats commenced firing just after 3:00 p.m., and the battery of Spanish cannons at McClure's Hill joined in. The cannons of Fort San Carlos defended Amelia Island against the Spanish assault, with Irwin's forces inflicting casualties on Spanish troops that were concentrated below McClure's Hill, destroying a portion of their cannon powder supply; however, firing continued until dark. The commander of Spanish forces, convinced he could not capture the island or force Irwin to yield, was forced to withdraw, leaving Fernandina and the island in the hands of Irwin and Hubbard.

Luis Aury, a privateer who was waging war for Mexican independence from Spain, was the next to take control of Fernandina. He blockaded the harbor with three ships and prevented the Spanish from regaining control of the town by sea or through the Intercoastal Waterway. With a force of over one hundred men and money to support the resistance, Aury was the next to assume control of the island and town, raising the Mexican rebel flag. His occupation was short-lived, as the United States could not allow a privateer to control the waters between Saint Marys, Georgia, and Fernandina, Florida. As a result, in December 1817, U.S. military forces once again occupied Fernandina and held it until Spanish forces could gain full occupation, thus forcing Aury to leave.

Under the Adams-Onis Treaty of 1819, Spain sold Florida to the United States for the sum of $5 million in 1821. Florida, then a U.S. territory, was open for settlement. Over the course of twenty years, several major events took place within the territory of Florida and on Amelia Island. The United States Army Corps of Engineers conducted an intensive survey of Florida, mapping its coastlines, rivers, inlets and inland territories and waterways. The port of Fernandina was one of the country's new major seaports, and the government looked to increase the infrastructure to facilitate increased ship traffic. In 1839, the Amelia Island Lighthouse was constructed, along with improved navigation beacons to direct ship traffic. The United States Customs Service was established at the port, and the U.S. Coast Guard and U.S. Revenue Service conducted operations in the waterways around Fernandina. The town was growing; it offered churches, schools, homes, workshops and ship chandleries with the many items that vessels needed for continued operations on the seas. Fernandina was a prized seaport since it was only one mile from the open ocean and offered a large deepwater harbor with common waters for ship anchorage. A natural deepwater channel that was able to accommodate any vessel afloat made Fernandina an attractive seaport; it had seventeen feet of draft at low tide and twenty-five feet of draft at high tide. Ships from all over the world made Fernandina an attractive seaport to visit.

In 1842, the U.S. government purchased tracts of land on the northern end of the island, about one and a half miles from the Old Town, and in 1847, Fort Clinch was built to provide protection for the major seaport of Fernandina and Saint Marys, Georgia. The War of 1812 had proved America's inability to defend its major seaports and waterways, as the British had been able to block the harbors in Baltimore, New York, Chesapeake and New Orleans. With a system of forts constructed prior to 1812, improved defenses were urgently needed to secure the new nation from foreign threats. The United States Corps of Engineers conducted multiple studies of the Fernandina's harbor and associated waterways and determined that it needed a strong fortress to insure its protection.

In 1856, the construction of the Florida Railroad increased use of the port of Fernandina, resulting in the growth of the town. Due to this growth, U.S. senator David L. Yulee, along with other local leaders, believed the location of Fernandina Old Town could not support the major changes the railroad business would bring. A new Fernandina was plotted two miles south of Old Town, along the Amelia River. It offered many of the same amenities as Old Town but provided more land to expand. New Fernandina was on its way to becoming a cosmopolitan city, with all the fanfare of the coastal cities to its North.

By 1860, the population of Amelia Island, including both Old and New Fernandina, had grown to 1,400 citizens, and its residents held the ideals of limited government and favored the right of states to oversee their needs and the rights of citizens to hold and keep property without the interference of the president or the U.S. government. The citizens were beginning to feel their options were becoming limited, and although they hoped for a peaceful separation from the federal union, the president's action and his stand of preserving the Union at all costs made it increasingly difficult to resolve the matter.

With an announcement from the railroad telegraph office that Florida had voted to secede from the federal union, Fernandina celebrated its new independence. Its independence was short-lived; by March 3, 1862, residents were forced to leave their beloved Fernandina and escape the federal invasion and occupation that followed. The federal capture of both towns and Fort Clinch added another chapter to the history of Amelia Island. From March 3, 1862, to June 30, 1865, the federal army and navy made great use of the towns and the fort as part of their vital operations in the area.

With the end of the war, Fernandina was spared the destruction that many towns and cities in the South endured. During Reconstruction, the United States military occupied Fernandina and Fort Clinch until the summer of 1869; it maintained law and order until the city government could be reestablished and operate with little assistance. With the end of slavery, a new chapter for former slaves became a part of postwar Fernandina history. In addition, many former federal soldiers that served on Amelia Island looked to start a new life in the place where they had recently been stationed. The Confederate veterans and citizens who left Fernandina in 1862 began returning to rebuild the lives they had before the Civil War began. Once enemies, veterans from the North and South worked together to grow Fernandina and bring it into its grand golden era.

1

SOUTHERN CALL TO ARMS

On December 20, 1861, South Carolina announced its secession from the United States, and on January 9, 1861, Mississippi followed suit. Florida became the third southern state to leave the Union; on January 10, 1861, Florida's delegates voted sixty-two to seven to withdraw. The delegates assembled at the state capital in Tallahassee to attend the state's constitutional convention, which began on January 3. Joseph Finegan and James Cooper represented Nassau County and the towns of Fernandina at the convention; both men voted for Florida to leave the Union.

Joseph Finegan, a prominent citizen of Fernandina, was employed with the Florida Railroad as a construction engineer and came to Fernandina to assist in overseeing the construction of the railroad. He owned a productive sawmill in Jacksonville, Florida, and assisted with work on the Atlantic and Gulf Railroads. While living in Fernandina, Finegan became involved in local politics, which led him to be selected as a representative of Nassau County, where he participated in Florida's vote to secede from the Union.

In 1860, Joseph Finegan was voted captain of the Fernandina Volunteers, the town's local militia company. Just before South Carolina seceded from the union on December 20, 1860, Finegan sent the following letter to the mayor of the city of Charleston, South Carolina, offering assistance.

Fernandina
Decb 18ᵗʰ, 1860
Hon Charles H Machith
Mayor City of Charleston

At a recent meeting of the Fernandina Volunteers, which I have the honor of commanding, the following resolution was unanimously adapted: that, should it become necessary for the authorities of South Carolina to rise force to obtain possession of the forts in Charleston Harbor, a detachment from this company, consisting of twenty-five men or more volunteers, be authorized to represent this company on that occasion and that the baptism of this company do enter in to the necessary co. and take the proper steps to secure to the said detachment the privilege of participating in said operation. In compliance with the above resolutions, I have the honor to report to you and thru you to the officer commanding in Charleston that a detachment of twenty-five men from this company are now ready to go to Charleston at a moment's warning, and I have to especially request that they be permitted the privilege on participating in any operations contemplated against the forts in your harbor. Hoping that our service will be accepted and requesting a reply at an early date.

I have the honor very respectful,
Joseph Finegan
Capt., commanding Fernandina Volunteers[1]

Florida's governor, Madison Starke Perry, in response to South Carolina and Mississippi's secession from the Union, called on the state militia forces to assemble in order to seize Fort Clinch in Fernandina, four forts in Pensacola, four in the Florida Keys (three at Key West and one in the Gulf of Mexico), one at Saint Augustine, the U.S. Navy Yard at Pensacola and the federal arsenal in Gadsden County that was known as the Apalachicola Arsenal.

Governor Perry believed these U.S. military sites were state property and should be used by the state forces to defend the citizens of Florida. With his term as governor ending in October 1861, Perry took actions to defend Florida's independence. Following the end of his term as Florida's governor, Perry went on to serve in the state and Confederate army as the colonel of Seventh Regiment Florida Infantry. However, in June 1863, with his health declining, Perry was forced to resign from the regiment and Confederate army and returned to Florida, where he lived until his death in March 1865.

Left: Joseph Finegan commanded the Fernandina Volunteers in 1861, becoming a general in the Confederate army. *Courtesy of the State Archives of Florida.*

Right: Governor Madison S. Perry called on the state's militia forces to seize Florida's U.S. arsenals and forts. *Courtesy of the State Archives of Florida.*

On January 2, 1861, United States senators David L. Yulee and Stephen R. Mallory sent a letter to the U.S. War Department requesting a record of ordnance and quartermaster supplies at the United States forts and arsenals located within the state. Senator Yulee was a prominent citizen of Fernandina and was the builder of the Florida Railroad that connected Fernandina on the east coast with Cedar Key on the west coast. As a U.S. senator representing Florida, Yulee helped Florida become a state in March 1845, and he lobbied the U.S. government to construct fortifications to secure and defend the state's major seaports and waterways, including Fernandina. Yulee, who was no longer a U.S. senator and who did not hold any formal position within the Confederate government, was offered to serve as an advisor to the governors of Florida; he served both Madison S. Perry (until the expiration of his term) and John Milton. During the last years of the war, Yulee went on to assist President Jefferson Davis. After he was captured in 1865 by federal forces, Yulee was imprisoned at Fort Pulaski near Savannah, Georgia, until 1866.

Madison Stark Perry, the governor during Florida's secession from the union, reinstated the state militia forces in 1858, requiring all males

19

U.S. senator David Yulee, a driving force in Florida becoming a state and later seceding from the union. *Courtesy of the State Archives of Florida.*

between the ages of eighteen to forty-five to enroll in a militia unit or be fined a state militia tax. In 1858, the town of Fernandina organized the Minute Men, a force made up of Fernandina and Nassau County residents. In November 1860, the militia changed its name to the Fernandina Volunteers, and as such, its members were required to attend regular monthly gatherings at the county seat in New Town Fernandina. The selected uniforms were blue flannel shirts, gray jean trousers and white leather cross belts.

> *The head wear is a mix of sort, for you can tell your neighbor by his hat. For me, a wide brim greatly keeps the sun off my neck and face for when we stand together doing nothing and our officers look over their book of instruction to tell us what to do.*
> —*militia member Thomas H. Broome*[2]

The officers and noncommissioned officers were elected for two years from 1860 to 1862. The men of the company voted Joseph Finegan as their captain, Henry C. Dozier and Felix Livingston as first lieutenants and J.S. Snow as second lieutenant. The militia was trained in the infantry tactics of the day and carried out various duties, working together in what one member described as "getting along."

We drill twice a day in the early morning and afternoon. Around before supper time, the drills are generally kept to an hour, with simple detail of arms and marching. The men who have business are concerned that a sale will miss them by if not opened on time in the morning.
—militia member Felix Livingston[3]

In addition to the Fernandina Volunteers, the Jefferson Davies Rifles were organized by the citizens of Nassau county in February 1861. George W. Call was elected by the prominent citizens of Fernandina to command the Davies Rifles, as they were sometimes called. Along with being the attorney for the Florida Railroad and a state legislator, Call commanded the Davies Rifles until the unit was recruited to join other Florida regiments in October 1861. Call went on to serve with the Second Regiment Florida Infantry as a captain and later as a major. During the Battle of Seven Pines, while leading a counterattack, Major George Call was killed. His body was brought home and laid to rest in Jacksonville, Florida.

To maintain an open seaport for Fernandina, the state's next course of action was to construct artillery batteries. The construction of Fort Clinch, which was located just three miles from New Town, was started in the fall of 1847 and continued for fourteen years. When the militia arrived, the only quarters in the fort were the guardroom, the prison and the carpenter shops. Only two walls had been built to their full height along with the north bastion, and the remaining portions of the fort were in various stages of construction. To make matters worse, the ramparts were incomplete and unable to support cannons, and there were no cannons at the fort that could be used to defend the waterway.

On January 3, 1861, in an effort to overcome this obstacle, the Fernandina Volunteers traveled sixty miles down the coast to St. Augustine and Fort Marion, an old Spanish fort that was renamed after Frances Marion in 1821, the swamp fox leader of the American forces and hero of the Revolutionary War. Upon arriving at the fort, which was serving as a storage place for military supplies, the Fernandina Volunteers found artillery, small arms and ammunition, including a field battery of 4 six-pounder guns, 2 twelve-pounder howitzers, 20 sea coast and garrison cannons, 4 eight-inch howitzers, 16 thirty-two-pounders, 6 six-pounders, old iron guns, 31 foreign cannons, 2,021 projectiles, 330 rounds of fixed ammunition, 873 priming tubes, 931 pounds of cannon powder, 110 muskets, 107 rifles, 103 Halls rifles and carbines, 98 pistols, 147,720 small arm cartridges and 15,000 percussion caps. Of the large quantity of ordnance stores, the Fernandina

Securing military provisions for Fernandina, the Fernandina Volunteers removed artillery, guns and ammunition from Fort Marion in Saint Augustine. *Courtesy of the State Archives of Florida.*

Volunteers transported 10 heavy caliber cannons and a large supply of artillery ammunition back to Fernandina. Of the 10 cannons that were brought back, 7 were thirty-two-pounders and 3 were twenty-four-pounders. These were transported along with a battery of 4 light six-pound field guns, muskets, pistols and small arms ammunition. The steam ship *Everglade* transported the ordnance stores, which were delivered to Fort Clinch and New Town Fernandina.

On March 10, 1861, the Palatka Guard arrived on Amelia Island, and with their arrival came the creation of the Jefferson Davis Rifles of Nassau County, a second militia company in addition to the Fernandina Volunteers. The state militia, which was then under the command of Lieutenant Colonel William Butler, totaled 270 officers and men. Colonel Butler directed the

22

construction of batteries, realizing it would be impossible to mount cannons in Fort Clinch. It was almost time for the militia to move toward formally occupying Fort Clinch, as the fort had been secured verbally but not occupied by state forces on a large scale.

During March 1861, Captain David P. Woodbury from the United States Army Corps of Engineers was sent to Fernandina to settle the accounts in relation to Fort Clinch for the U.S Government. Colonel Butler informed Captain Woodbury that any sale would be illegal, and the state claimed ownership of the Fort. In a letter dated April 2, 1861, Captain Woodbury stated to his superiors:

General,

I have the honor to report my return from Fort Clinch and my performance of the duty assigned to me by your order of the 18th Ultimo, so far as I have been able to perform it. I have paid off all employees mentioned in Captain Whiting's letter 8th Ultimo and discharged all not before discharged, except the fort keeper Mr. J.A. walker and two laborers, partly because the sand embankments inside the fort required constant attention and partly because I was not able to sell any of the public property.

After I had paid off the accounts, Colonel Butler, commanding the Florida militia at Fernandina, very politely informed me that the authorities of that state had virtually taken possession of Fort Clinch and that any sale of its property by the United States would be regarded as illegal and that he thought it his duty to resist such sale if necessary. After some conversation, finding myself unable to change his resolution, I was, of course, compelled to yield.

The state of Florida, or the Confederate states, will probably soon take formal possession of Fort Clinch. I have told Mr. Walker that, while things remain as they are, he may regard himself and his assistants as in the service of the United States, at least until he shall be officially informed to the contrary, but that whenever the property or the fort shall be actually seized, the United States will be no longer responsible for services. There are some small accounts for supplies and for services still unpaid. As soon as I receive them, I will forward them to the department for your decision.

Respectfully,
D.P. Woodbury
captain, engineers[4]

On the morning of April 8, 1861, the Fernandina Volunteers, along with the Palatka Guard and Jefferson Davis Rifles, marched along the Fort Clinch military road that connected Old Fernandina with the fort. They arrived at the site by late morning and encountered J.A. Walker, the fort caretaker, and two workmen. Mr. Walker advised the militia commanders that he and his workers were the only men in the fort and that they were employed to complete the sodding of the ramparts under the direction of Captain Woodbury from the U.S. Corps of Engineers. This work was assigned by Captain Whiting, the engineer officer in charge of the fort's construction before he left to join the Confederate army. Woodbury directed Walker to continue his work as it had previously been assigned to him.

A small ceremony was held with a few special statements by Colonel Butler, and the town leaders accompanied the militia to the fort. A small group of citizens witnessed the capture and occupation of the fort. Without a flagpole installed, the militia had the honor of erecting the first flagpole. With the Fernandina cadets playing their fifes and drums, the first flag to ever fly over Fort Clinch, a white bunting flag with a blue six-pointed star in the middle and the words "Hurrah for Florida, Let Us Alone," was raised. However, the flag was replaced in a short time by the state flag. With the raising of the flag, Fort Clinch was formally under the authority of the state and, within a few months, the Confederate States of America. With the formation of the Confederate States, the first national flag, with seven white stars on a blue field, two red stripes and one white stripe in the middle of the two red stripes, flew over Fernandina and Fort Clinch by the summer of 1861. It should be noted that at no time before the occupation of Fort Clinch by Florida militia forces did a flag fly over the fort. To recognize the Fernandina Volunteers, the ladies' society, led by Mrs. Dozier, the wife of Lieutenant Henry C. Dozier, presented the militia company with its very own flag made of white and blue silk with the seal of the state in the center and the words "Fernandina Volunteers God and Our Country." The reverse side had a gold wreath with thirteen stars in the center.

Our flags can be seen flying atop the tall homes and buildings of Fernandina and at the batteries and fort.
—militia member Felix Livingston[5]

Fernandina was a unique town, and although the majority of its population was prosouthern, a small group of citizens were in support of the federal government. Many moved to the state from the North in the prewar years,

The ladies of Fernandina present the Fernandina Volunteers with a flag in May 1861.
Courtesy of the collection of Dicky Ferry.

and for many, Florida was their home. They raised families, acquired land, opened businesses and supported the state, but their loyalty to the United States was firm. Approximately 10 percent of the state's male population was pro-Union and supported the nation's elected leaders and government. The laws of the state required the adult male population to enroll in the state militia forces, and these loyal men were caught in the secession of Florida.

One of the most interesting individual histories from Fernandina is that of Benjamin Thompson. After moving to Florida in the late 1850s, Thompson was employed as a teacher for Colonel R.F. Dancy's family. He resided in Orange Mills (Palatka) before moving to Jacksonville, where he worked as a shopkeeper for Samuel Ellis & Company. He then moved to Fernandina, where he ran the store that belonged to Mr. Ellis, and after two years, he became a partner in the business. Unfortunately, his co-owner passed away, and he found himself in a partnership with former governor James E. Broom. The business thrived and was quite successful.

As the election of President Lincoln was declared, Thompson became concerned because, as a member of the town's militia force, he and the other pro-Union citizens would be called up for state service, especially if Florida seceded from the Union. As anticipated, this occurred on January 10, 1861. The state militia was then called into service by Governor Perry, and Thompson found himself with the Fernandina Volunteers, believing that it was best for all pro-Union men to be placed into one militia company. Thompson and the others were able to petition to create a company of artillery, and they recruited fifty men to handle the artillery brought back from Saint Augustine. Their uniforms were similar to those of the original Fernandina Volunteers, but theirs had an additional bright red flannel trouser stripe denoting artillery. The company had a "go as you please" discipline; once, Thompson described, while towing a cannon via scow, the volunteers' captain called out to one of them riding on the scow and asked:

> *Garvin, are not you able to pull on the rope. Garvin replied, "Perfectly able, Captain, but not willing."*
> —*militia member Benjamin Thompson*[6]

As time went on, the reorganization of the militia companies occurred. To remain as an independent company, they were required to have seventy men, and in order to meet this requirement they began recruiting. In a short time, they had the required number. Thompson was very much a citizen of Fernandina and Florida, as he had purchased land, operated a business, served on the city council and was an elder in the church he helped to build in Fernandina. However, his view of Florida's separation from the Union and his love for the United States eventually forced him and others to leave the state and defend the country instead of taking up arms against it. Since he was unable to abruptly quit the militia, he worked to disband the group; in the spring of 1861, Thompson managed to leave Fernandina.

However, things were not easy for Thompson; as a known southern citizen, he was met with a group of angry citizens who were intending to cause him harm as he boarded a steamship heading for Savannah. Thompson was fearful for his safety until, in a moment of surprise, former senator David L. Yulee appeared, walked the docks, boarded the steamship and took a seat on the upper deck, where the crowd could see him. Yulee's presence calmed the angry crowd, and Thompson, his sister and the other pro-Union folks were able to board the vessel and leave. Benjamin W. Thompson eventually made his way back to New York and went on the serve in the federal army. In a unique series of events, he became the provost marshal for the federal army's Department of the South, which was stationed in Hilton Head, South Carolina. In 1865, as the provost marshal, Thompson was the military jailer of former Senator Yulee, the same man who helped Thompson leave Fernandina in 1861. In August 1973, *The Civil War Times Illustrated* published Thompson's full story.

As was expected, the women and children of Fernandina were caught up in the secessionist movement, with young girls making items for the many southern troops that occupied the towns. Parades and social events were all the rage in Fernandina, and they were organized by the ladies' society of the town. Many social groups supported the troops with sewing societies, including the Lady's Relief Society and the Lady's Society for Soldiers and Sailors. Young boys under the age of eighteen were eager to serve as well, which made way for the formation of the Fernandina Cadets, which was commanded by Captain Ford Finegan. The Fernandina Cadets assisted in moving cannons, working wagons of supplies to equip the troops, conducting water rations for the militia forces stationed around the island and serving in the fife and drum corps. The citizens were very involved in supporting the Confederate troops and were sure that the war would soon be won and that the South would be its own nation. They were so confident in this that they even used school funds to buy arms and ammunition along with other pressing articles that were needed to support the cause of southern independence and their army.

On August 5, 1861, the Fernandina lookouts spotted the merchant ship *Alvarado* making its way toward the main shipping channel with a cargo of wool, hides, copper and medical supplies. Following at a distance behind the *Alvarado* was a United States warship, also known as a sloop, called the USS *Jamestown*. The *Jamestown*, which was constructed between 1843 to 1844 and commissioned in January 1845 weighed 985 tons, was 163 feet long and 36 feet wide. The sloop was armed with twenty guns, six eight-inch cannons and fourteen thirty-two pounders.

For two months, the ships of the U.S. Navy patrolled the waters off the coasts of South Carolina, Georgia and Florida. Hoping to make a prize of the *Alvarado*, the *Jamestown* moved in to capture the vessel. The assembly "call to arms" was sounded throughout Fernandina, and the troops began a rapid movement toward the east side of the island, where the militia forces had four bronze six-pounder field cannons; two of them were posted at Fort Clinch, and the other two were stationed in New Fernandina. The citizens raced along the shell road to the beach, where they gathered to watch the events unfold. The captain of the *Alvarado*, unable to outsail

In August 1861, the merchant ship *Alvarado* was beached off Fernandina and burned to prevent capture by the USS *Jamestown*. *Courtesy of the State Archives of Florida.*

the *Jamestown* and wanting to prevent the cargo from being captured, made the decision to beach the ship and scuttle it. The event was the great excitement of the summer, with the militia forces attempting to render assistance to the *Alvarado*.

With their two six-pounders, the militia forces began firing on the advancing USS *Jamestown*; however, they were unsuccessful in scoring any hits on the warship. With the *Alvarado* beached just two miles north of what is known today as Fernandina's Main Beach and just a mile and a half from Fort Clinch, the *Jamestown* sent a boarding party consisting of three launches. The first launch had four navy officers, seventeen sailors and eight marines. The second launch had two officers, sixteen sailors and five marines. The third launch had midshipman Tyson and a party of twelve men with orders from Jamestown's commander, Captain Green, to set fire to the ship if they were unable to make the *Alvarado* a prize "captured ship." With the boarding parties now approaching the *Alvarado* and with the two six-pounders from Fort Clinch arriving to fire on the enemy, the militia tried to set up a crossfire on the approaching boats. The artillery crew concentrated their fire on the boarding party boats with the hopes of forcing the enemy to abandon its attempt to board the *Alvarado*. The position set up by the militia was somewhat hopeless, as the boarding boats were able to move in behind the *Alvarado* and avoid the artillery fire. The scene on the beach was one of great excitement, with nearly two hundred people, including senator Yulee, witnessing the action. Unable to stop the U.S. Navy, the *Alvarado* was set on fire. This event was the result of the town's citizens and the militia coming together to defend the cause they were involved in: attempting to save the ship. The loss of the *Alvarado* was only a sign of what was to occur along the coast of Florida. Over the course of the summer of 1861, more southern troops began to arrive in Fernandina. By the end of July, the southern forces consisted of ten small militia companies, which numbered about seventy officers and men each. The companies had the most colorful names: Wakulla Guard, Hernando Guard, Madison Gray Eagles, Dixie Stars, Suwannee Guards, Fernandina Volunteers, Jefferson Rifles, Davis Guards, Jefferson Davis Rifles and Fernandina Cadets. The force totals were as follows: 1 lieutenant colonel, 1 quartermaster, 1 commissary, 4 captains, 3 first lieutenants, 8 second lieutenants, 1 surgeon, 17 sergeants, 20 corporals, 4 musicians and 379 privates. All of them were present for duty. On the sick list and not present for duty were 30 enlisted men and 6 officers; 1 officer and 45 enlisted men were listed as absent with leave, and 2 enlisted men were listed as absent without leave.

A portion of the Third Regiment Florida Infantry arrived at the end of July, and Colonel William S. Dilworth of the Third Florida Regiment, who was appointed the commanding officer of all the state troops serving on Amelia Island, replaced Lieutenant Colonel Butler. With the arrival of the Third Florida, the number of troops numbers increased to over six hundred. Unimpressed with the defenses of Fernandina and Amelia Island, Colonel Dilworth sent his concerns and requests in a letter to the Confederate government in Richmond.

August 12, 1861
Richmond, VA
To the Honorable J. Norton, G.T. Ward, J.B. Owens, or L.P. Walker,

Dear Sir, having been recently elected and commissioned colonel of this regiment, I ask that you give your attention to the following views. I have six companies of infantry on this island, two at the mouth of the Saint John's and two at Saint Augustine. On this island, there is a sort of battery, but incomplete. The guns, four in number, six-pounders, are badly mounted and would not stand continued firing. I regard the battery and guns a very little protection, I have heard that forty thirty-two-pounders were ordered over here, also a competent engineer. I hope this is so. They will satisfy our wishes on this point. Our companies here are composed of from eight to one hundred men, more than enough to manage the guns at the battery, while their other duties in guarding the coast will give them ample employment. I would, therefore, ask that I be allowed to raise an artillery company of sixty-four men, which should be attached to this regiment. This company I could raise in a very short time. But more important to the defense of this island than anything is a company of dragoons or mounted men. This island has a seacoast stretching along the Atlantic eighteen miles in length, at any point of which the enemy could land any number of troops in surf boats. The enemy's war vessels are in sight every day; one supposed to be the Vincennes, having on Monday burned a prize within a mile and half of the shore. They also anchored on last Thursday evening within two miles of the shore, opposite this town, making the distance, land and water, from the town three and a half miles. Now, if I had a horse company, I could protect the sea beach, and they could not land without my being in so to meet them at the place of landing. With a cavalry company, I could dispose my infantry as to meet them, the enemy, at almost any point they may attempt to land; but with only six companies on this island, placing one of these at the battery, then you have five infantry companies to protect and guard a coast of eighteen or twenty miles. I hope, therefore, that a company of dragoons will be allowed me in addition to what I have to command. I regard this as absolutely necessary to our proper defense and ask to refer you to a report which Captain McRory has furnished at my request, he having been captain of a volunteer artillery company on the island. I have not as yet visited the mouth of the Saint John's or Saint Augustine; this regiment only having been organized on the 11th instant. As soon as I can see those places, I will, if necessary, report their condition. One more suggestion: I think the George and Florida Atlantic ought to be placed under one command, the nature and character of defenses necessary.

I have no drill officer. My regiment is composed entirely of citizens. I would be glad to have two drill officers attached to this regiment immediately. If I cannot have them sent here, I could engage them here if I had the authority. Be pleased to attend to this without delay, and believe me, yours respectfully,

Colonel W.S. Dilworth
Commanding[7]

In response to the letter from Colonel Dilworth, the Confederate War Department sent the following letter.

War Department, CSA,
Richmond, August 19, 1861

Colonel, W.S. Dilworth
Fernandina, FL

Sir, attention of this department has been already directed to the importance of the defense of the harbor of Fernandina, and in reply to your letter of the 12th instant, I have the honor to inform you that artillery such as you desire has been already directed to be forwarded to you, in compliance with requisitions addressed to this department, and it is hoped it may arrive in time to meet your most pressing exigencies. In reply to the further proposition, I have the honor to say that an artillery company, if organized and furnished with a battery, will be accepted, and assigned to your command if its services are desired by you, and that a cavalry company also armed and furnishing its own horses, will be accepted, if required, and assigned to your command.

Respectfully,
L.P. Walker
Secretary of War[8]

By September 1861, three additional cannons, two eight-inch Columbiads and one six-inch rifle, arrived, along with four companies of the First Florida Special Battalion under the command of Lieutenant Colonel D.P. Holland. Confederate forces on the island numbered just over one thousand; the officers and men serving at Fernandina and Fort Clinch served in six militia companies, a portion of the Third Regiment Florida Infantry and four companies of the First Florida Special Battalion.

To oversee the various commands in Florida, the Department of Middle and East Florida was created. Brigadier General John B. Grayson was then placed in command of Middle and East Florida. Grayson graduated from the Military Academy at West Point in 1826 and served in the Florida's Indian Wars and the Mexican War of 1846–1848, for which he received two brevets for gallantry and meritorious conduct. He had thirty-five years of service in the United States Army and served in three branches, the artillery,

With Fort Clinch under construction, Confederate forces found the fort ill-equipped to defend the waterway and surrounding area. *Courtesy of the State Archives of Florida.*

quartermaster and commissary corps, and he held the rank of lieutenant colonel before resigning from the U.S. Army on July 1, 1861, to join the Confederate army.

During the months of September and October, General Grayson conducted military inspections of Middle and East Florida. He was unimpressed with Fernandina and its defenses and ordered the construction of additional artillery batteries and improvements to be made to those that were already built. As he traveled by train across the only landward side of the island, Grayson was surprised to see no fortifications to render a defense to the trestle bridge; the only way to leave the island if unable to travel by boat. Grayson immediately ordered the batteries increase their current number of cannons.

For the sand and palm log battery southeast of Fort Clinch, the cannons were increased to ten and quite possibly twenty. The Cumberland Island battery at the south end, overlooking the sound, was increased from six to eight cannons. Old Town Fernandina, along with New Town, constructed a battery for two cannons, and the railroad trestle bridge also had an artillery position to mount two or three cannons along with a mortar. Recognizing the need to defend the southern end of Amelia Island, a battery of four field cannons was placed; since the waterway was very shallow and only a small boat with a draft of about five feet could enter, a large artillery position was not required. Instead, a battery of field artillery could cover the entrances to Nassau Sound. In a report to Richmond, Grayson expressed his concerns that cannon powder was urgently needed, along with additional artillery and other military supplies, for the command at Fernandina. He said if the items were not sent, it was possible that Fernandina would fall into enemy hands.

To oversee the new artillery position, Frances Shoupe was selected and commissioned a lieutenant. Shoupe, a West Point graduate, served in the United States Army Artillery Corps from 1855 to 1860; after resigning from the U.S. army, he practiced law in St. Augustine. Lieutenant Shoupe directed the renewed efforts to construct the required artillery positions ordered by General Grayson.

The cannon positions located southeast of Fort Clinch were dismantled, and a ten-gun battery was built with room for more artillery, should it arrive. Two new positions were planned for both towns, and another position was planned for the railroad trestle bridge. On the south end of Cumberland Island, the orders were the same, with an increase of artillery to six or eight cannons. This project was a massive undertaking; however, it was needed to ensure the protection of the waterways and an open port in Fernandina. Lieutenant Shoupe was nearing completion on the batteries when orders arrived reassigning him to other duties. After leaving Fernandina, Shoupe was promoted in the Confederate army and became a brigadier general by the war's end.

To handle the lack of accommodations at Fort Clinch, the Confederate troops established camps in and around the fort. *Courtesy of the collection of Dicky Ferry.*

The following request for artillery was made to Richmond by General Grayson; he had the sincere hope that much of the listed items would be sent to Amelia Island: fourteen thirty-two-pounders, six of which should be rifled; four forty-two-pounders, also to be rifled; twenty-three thousand pounds of cannon powder; twelve thousand musket cartridges; and three hundred rounds of ammunition for the field cannons. With every Confederate state requiring military ordnance and supplies, Florida was not at the top of the list; however, by October 30, 1861, the adjutant and inspector general, F.L. Dancy, sent a report to Governor John Milton on the current deposition of artillery, ammunition and conduct of the troops of Fernandina.

ADJUTANT AND INSPECTOR GENERAL'S OFFICE
Tallahassee, FL, October 30, 1861
His Excellency John Milton, governor of Florida:

Sir: In obedience to your instruction of the 16ʰ instant, requiring me to visit Fernandina and report to you the condition of the defenses at that place, I have the honor to submit the following, viz: The defenses consist of a sand and palmetto-log battery of eight guns, all mounted, to wit: five 32-pounders, two 24-pounders (smooth bore), and one rifle 6-inch gun on ship carriage. This battery I conceive to be very injudiciously arranged, having 24-pounders, 32-pounders, and rifle guns all in the same battery in barbette, except that two of the 32-pounders are partially masked by slight traverses on the parapet. These traverses confine the field of fire seaward to about 15 degrees. These guns are all placed on a straight line, except the rifled gun, which is placed just in rear of the left gun, and when fired its direction, will be obliquely over the short-range guns, thereby endangering the men at these guns, and at the same time, drawing the fire of the enemy on the whole battery long before they come within the reach of the 24-pounders and 32-pounders. There is also one 24-pounder and two 32-pounders unmounted at Fort Clinch, and one 8-inch Columbiad landed at the wharf at Fernandina on the 27ʰ instant.

The weather during my visit was so stormy as to render it impossible for me to visit Colonel Holland's camp at the south end of the island, 18 miles distant; neither did I witness the drill of the troops in the immediate vicinity of Fernandina for the same reason; but the idea formed by seeing the men and officers about the streets was anything but favorable to their discipline, having seen several staggering through the streets on the sabbath day. They are sadly in want of an efficient commander and a good drill master, both artillery and infantry. I learned that Colonel Holland had not yet located his permanent camp at the south end of the island; neither had any breast works been thrown up, having but a few days before moved to that point. His command consists of four companies of artillery, with four brass 6-pounders, 500 6-pound balls, and 75 grape and canister, and 500 cannon friction tubes, his men are armed with muskets and carbines—4,000 caps, and a lot of balls. Of ammunition, as far as I could learn, there are 300 32-pounder caps, 500 cannon friction tubes, 770 32-pound balls, 80 32-pound shells, 100 rounds of shell and fixed ammunition for the 32-pounder rifled gun, 90 24-pound balls, 12,000 ball and buck-shot cartridges, 12,000 caps (the latter-balls and caps delivered to the officer in command of the fort), 7,000 caps still in possession of General Finegan. The above constitutes, as far as I could learn, all the ammunition on the island.

There are, at this time, seven companies on the island, one of which is a cavalry company and the others are infantry. These are exclusive of the four companies belonging to Colonel Holland's battalion of artillery. This battalion has never been mustered into either state or Confederate service, but an order for them to be furnished with the requisite arms and equipments issued by General Grayson has been forwarded to Richmond, showing the amount necessary to place this battalion in condition for active and efficient service.

Respectfully, your obedient servant,
F.L. Dancy
adjutant and inspector general[9]

On October 21, 1861, Brigadier John B. Grayson passed away, with Brigadier General James Heyward Trapier assuming command. Like his predecessor, Trapier attended the United States Military Academy at West Point and graduated third of his class in 1838. Upon graduation, he served in the corps of engineers and later served in the artillery. After resigning in 1848 to become a planter, he was commissioned in the Confederate army with the rank of brigadier general and was placed in command of Middle and East Florida until April 1862.

Like General Grayson, Trapier had serious concerns about the defenses at Fernandina, which he addressed with Governor John Milton and General Robert E. Lee, the commander of the Department of South Carolina, Georgia and Florida. Trapier pressed the issue of providing a strong defense

Five artillery batteries were constructed to defend Amelia Island; altogether, they had thirty-three cannons of various sizes and types. *Courtesy of the State Archives of Florida.*

of the Cumberland Sound and associated waterways. Although the troops and artillery had increased, the vital ammunition had not. Another concern General Trapier had was for the mustering of Florida's forces at Fernandina into the army of the Confederate States of America, which allowed for the receiving of military supplies and equipment from the government stores.

Not all the units had been sworn into the Confederacy; in Fernandina, only two units had officially been mustered in. The First Florida Battalion was accepted for state service by the late General Grayson, but a matter arose when the battalion of artillery was mustered in, since general artillery is mustered in as a battery, not as a battalion. The matter was somewhat interesting, in that, if the First Florida Battalion was not accepted, they would head to Georgia and be mustered in there; however, the issue was resolved, and the battalion was accepted for Confederate service. In the case of the militia companies, their men were accepted into Florida infantry, cavalry and artillery units that were then serving at Fernandina. Many of the Fernandina Volunteers, along with men from various militia units, were mustered into the Second, Third and Fourth Florida Infantry Regiments, along with the First Florida Special Battalion.

November saw the arrival of the Marion Light Artillery, which was commanded by Captain John M. Martin and had four six-pounders and 106 men. This unit arrived with the Marion Dragoons, which were under the command of Captain William A. Owens and had 110 men. Additional supplies were also making their way to Fernandina; they included sabers, muskets, small arms ammunition and five heavy cannons. By December 1861, the monthly report for the Department of Middle and East Florida listed the following confederate forces: the Third and Fourth Florida Infantry, the First Florida Special Battalion, the Twenty-Fourth Mississippi Infantry, Owen's Independent Troop, Martin's Light Battery and Baya's Company of Artillery, which was serving at Fernandina and Fort Clinch. The number of troops numbered 4,527, both present and absent, within the department.

Contracts were established with businesses and farms in the area to provide the troops with food and lodging. Mr. M. Wood & Company of Callahan, Florida, was contracted to supply the Confederate forces at Fernandina and Fort Clinch with beef rations. Mr. C.L. Holbrook provided pork and dry goods, and vegetables were under contract with various merchants from Fernandina and St. Marys, Georgia. Meals among the troops were enjoyable and, at the time, plentiful. In his journal, T.H. Broome wrote:

> *The rations which we receive each day are of the best quality available to us; we have beef three times a week with pork and fish, oyster, clams and crab, along with rice, onion and yams. The corn are right fine; our bread ration comes from the many bakers of the town, with our own mess providing biscuits and sweet bread. Wild game is abundant, but the troops are prevented from hunting them on the account of the ammunition's shortages. The weather allows for us to fish when not posted to duty at the fort or in the town; the citizens are always offering biscuits, sweet bread and cookes. My friends and neighbors are always visiting the men of the volunteers with treats and goodies.*
> —*militia member T.H. Broome*[10]

To accommodate the Confederate forces, three major military camps were established. Camp Jefferson, the largest camp, accommodated seven hundred soldiers and was named after President Jefferson Davis. It was located on the east side of New Fernandina on what was then known as the Shell Road, which connected the town to the beach and lighthouse on the east side of the Amelia Island. Camp Bartow, which held two hundred soldiers, was located between New and Old Town Fernandina on a high bluff overlooking the river to the west. Fort Clinch accommodated an encampment in front of the fort, with some men camped on the parade field within the fort. Small camps were located in the rear of the artillery

The towns of Fernandina supported the Confederate forces by providing lodging for the troops. *Courtesy of the State Archives of Florida.*

batteries on the island, with Camp Holland located on the south end of Amelia Island, thirteen miles from Fernandina. Officers were quartered with local families who extended their hospitality or rented rooms in various inns and homes. A camp was also established at the Amelia Island Lighthouse, which served as a lookout post.

With a population of 1,400 citizens before the arrival of Confederate forces, Fernandina's military population grew to almost 3,000. With additional Confederate forces arriving each month, the need for additional space presented the town with the opportunity to cut down the forest to the east and south, where new military camps were laid out for quarters to accommodate newly arrived troops.

There is much work here in the cutting down of the woods near the town to make a new camp. The trees are some of the largest in Fernandina. I have a saw and will be used to build quarters and provide cook wood; we have now some 300 men, with a group of slaves, working each day to make room for the army gathering here. Hope to have you visit soon. I am glad that I have a nice home to sleep in each night and do not have to sleep in a tent only when I am at the battery.
—militia member William C. Hagan.[11]

On December 21, 1861, Brigadier General James H. Trapier and his staff conducted a review of the Confederate forces at Amelia Island, Fernandina and Fort Clinch. The following troops were stationed at the various encampments and batteries, including Fort Clinch and the palm log and sand battery: portions of the Third and Fourth Florida Infantry, Old Town Fernandina, Marion Light Artillery, the Third Florida Infantry, New Town Fernandina, the Fourth Florida Infantry, Marion Dragoons, Railroad Bridge Battery, Captain William Baya's Grayson Artillery, (on horse patrol) Captain Williams Owen's troop of Marion Dragoons.

On December 25, 1861, the Confederate forces and citizens of Fernandina had a most joyous Christmas celebration. December 24 and 25 saw many social events, with the officers enjoying a wonderful feast hosted by the city's leaders and former governor Broome. A cotillion of music and dancing was held at many homes, and the enlisted men enjoyed an array of athletic activities and a theatrical play that was put on at the docks of Fernandina. The day was cold and pleasant, with hot cider and spicy drinks, wonderful fruit cakes, sweet bread and an assortment of baked goods. The senior officers enjoyed a social event hosted by former governor Broome with a fine serenade of carols by local children. The soldiers posted to duty received a visit by the ladies and children of the town, who presented small gifts of baked goods, cider and songs of the season. The Christmas of 1861 in Fernandina was a peaceful and joyous time, far from the war being fought in Virginia and Tennessee.

We had the most grandest event all over the island, from the finest dinners to the evening of singing and social engagements. Our citizens made the holiday an event to remember; only wishing I could have seen mother and father with you, my dear Helen. The war has not come to us here. It is said that the enemy is planning to attack up the coast, and if they are able to, they will come here next. The batteries are in a good position, and the men, including Peter and me, are well trained in the action of the guns.

—Confederate soldier William C. Hagan.[12]

As a new year started, the defenses of Amelia Island were in good order. The artillery batteries that former General Grayson had ordered to be constructed were fully completed by General Trapier and his troops, and the cannons were in place, with five main artillery positions. The cannons were mounted as follows: the south end of Cumberland Island Battery had six cannons, four thirty-two-pounders and two twenty-four-pounders; the Palm Log and Sand Battery, located southeast of Fort Clinch, had twelve cannons, four thirty-two-pounders, two eight-inch Columbiads, two twenty-four-pounders, one six-inch rifle gun, one thirty-two-pounder rifle gun and those unmounted at the battery, including one thirty-two-pounder and one rifled forty-two-pounder; Old Town Fernandina Battery had two twenty-four-pounders; New Town Fernandina had two twenty-four-pounders; and Railroad Bridge Battery had one eight-inch mortar and two thirty-two-pounders.

Fernandina had the largest concentration of Confederate forces in Northeast Florida by December 1861, with three thousand serving Confederates. *Courtesy of the State Archives of Florida.*

40

Located inside Fort Clinch were three unmounted cannons, two thirty-two-pounders one eight-inch Columbiad. Of the twenty-eight heavy cannons that were on Amelia Island, five were not installed and remained unmounted. In addition to the heavy artillery, a field battery of five cannons, four six-pounders and one three-inch gun, were available to the Confederate forces. The heavy artillery and field cannons brought the total to thirty-three cannons to ensure the defense of Amelia Island and the waterways.

As the appointed commander of Confederate forces for South Carolina, Georgia and Florida, General Robert E. Lee was responsible for overseeing the defenses of the state. From January 8 to 11, 1862, General Lee conducted a formal inspection of the defenses of Fernandina and its associated waterways. General Lee gave his approval of the battery positions and the arrangement of artillery. The defense was formidable, and the troops were satisfactory in the heavy artillery drill.

Captain Charles H. McBlair was no stranger to the operations of the United States military, as he had served in the U.S. Navy and attained the rank of commander before offering to serve the Confederate States of America. He was commissioned a captain in the provisional army of the Confederacy and was immediately placed in command of the batteries of Amelia and Cumberland Islands; he worked to improve the effectiveness of the artillery positions and make the needed requests for powder and ammunitions for his command. Under Brigadier James H. Trapier, Captain McBlair knew what was required to defend the waterways around the island and was determined to obtain the needed military stores. By January 1862, McBlair was advanced to the rank of colonel for his hard work and devotion to the defenses and was responsible for any and all matters associated with the batteries of both Cumberland and Amelia Island.

Captain McBlair, the commander of the batteries, advised General Lee that the island's current amount of ammunition was insufficient to withstand a continual firing of the batteries in a prolonged engagement with the U.S. Navy. The amount of cannon powder on hand totaled 10,000 pounds, along with only 1,200 friction primers to fire the artillery. General Lee was informed of the need for the necessary artillery supplies in addition to the lack of small arms munitions and accouterments. General Lee informed the commanders of Fernandina that other concerns also needed to be addressed.

The batteries north Amelia Island at Saint Simons, Jeckyl Island and Brunswick, Georgia, needed to guard the Intercoastal Waterway from being used by the enemy's navy, which received limited attention in the way of artillery and other supplies. Lee advised that the enemy, if possible, would make use of

The Sand and Palm Log Battery southeast of Fort Clinch was the largest artillery position, with ten mounted cannons. *Courtesy of the Library of Congress.*

the inland waterways at Brunswick and could take the position of the batteries from the rear and threaten the town of Fernandina. On January 15, 1862, General Lee sent a letter to the commander of Fernandina informing him that the needed supplies for the troops were being directed by Captain Cuyler of the ordnances corps. The following articles were listed as en route to Fernandina: five hundred sets of Enfield accouterments, with additional accouterments for infantry troops from the Augusta Arsenals consisting of three hundred sets; three hundred pairs of footwear and some clothing to come from Columbus Depot; for the artillery, two thousand pounds of powder and five hundred pounds of lead was to be made into small arms cartridges. Lee also informed the commander that Richmond was directing four eight-inch Columbiads to be sent to Fernandina along with additional cannon powder. General Robert E. Lee also stated that attempts were being made to defend the area in and around Saint Simons and Jeckyl Island, along with Brunswick, to block the enemy's navy from using the intercoastal waterways there.

At its height, the Confederate forces on Amelia Island totaled three thousand officers and enlisted men. It was the largest occupation of Confederate forces in Northeast Florida during the fall and winter of 1861, and this number did not grow again in Northeast Florida until the battle of Olustee on February 20, 1864, and the occupation at Camp Milton in Jacksonville, where eight thousand troops were stationed there following the Confederate victory over the federal forces at Olustee. In January 1862, Confederate troop numbers changed, and the following account of officers and enlisted men at Fernandina was reported: 777 from the Fourth Regiment Florida Infantry; 895 from the Twenty-Fourth Mississippi Infantry Regiment; 577 from the First Florida Battalion; 120 from the Marion Dragoons (Owen's Independent Troop); 110 from the Marion Light Artillery (Martin's Light Battery), 34 from Baya's Company of Artillery; and 45 from Simmon's Coast Guard. Several units were ordered to serve elsewhere in the state.

General Trapier reported that 4,680 officers and enlisted men were in the Department of Middle and East Florida, with the greatest number of troops located in Fernandina and at Fort Clinch. In addition to the number of troops at Fernandina, General Trapier's staff also consisted of twelve officers and eighteen enlisted men who served in the following positions: adjutant, quartermaster, commissary, ordnance, medical, chaplain, military aides and inspector general. The enlisted men served as messengers and security forces for the general and his staff. The commanders of Fernandina and Fort Clinch, from the time Florida withdrew from the Union, were: Captain Joseph Finegan (January 1861 to March 1861); Lieutenant Colonel William Butler (March 1861 to August 1861); Colonel William S. Dilworth (August 1861 to January 1862); and Colonel Edward Hopkins (January 1862 to the time Confederate forces abandoned Fernandina and Fort Clinch, with Colonel Charles H. McBlair serving as the commander of the batteries).

The commanding officers for the Department of Middle and East Florida were as follows: Brigadier General John B. Grayson (September 1861 to October 1861) and Brigadier General James H. Trapier (November 1861 to April 1862). After the Confederates abandoned Fernandina in April 1862, Joseph Finegan, the former commander of the Fernandina Volunteers and a prominent citizen, assumed command for the Department of Middle and East Florida, replacing General Trapier. Special Order No. 80 directed Finegan to report to Major General Pemberton for his assignment to take command of Middle and East Florida. General John B. Grayson died of pneumonia on October 21, 1861, just one month after assuming command of the department and carrying out an inspection of Fernandina's defenses.

Fernandina, both Old and New Town, was fortunate to have skilled doctors as citizens of the community, as it had a need for talented physicians who were able to care for the seaport and its many ships and mariner crews. With the arrival of Confederate forces and the monthly increase in their numbers since Florida's secession came a great need to attend to the medical needs of

Captain Charles McBlair, the commander of the artillery batteries for Amelia and Cumberland Islands, oversaw thirty-three cannons to defend the waterways. *Courtesy of the State Archives of Florida.*

the Confederate troops. With large numbers of soldiers came many types of sickness, including measles, chicken pox, pneumonia and the common cold. The most affected were young soldiers with a weak quality of health.

Dr. Charles White and Dr. Hollingsworth served as the primary physicians for the southern forces, with Dr. Henry L. Lungren as an assistant surgeon joining them later in 1861. Dr. White and Dr. Hollingsworth stated the troops were in good health at the end of the summer; however, with the arrival of fall, things changed. In a letter to his wife, Dr. Hollingsworth mentioned that about three men died each day during November, and many more were on bedrest with smallpox, measles and fever. The illnesses put one company of soldiers to bed, with only twenty-one available for duty. The officers were also under the weather, with eleven of them unable to command their men. It was a trick of fate that some of those men died before ever reaching the battlefield.

As February 1862 began, all the work completed to defend the waterways became a disappointment, as news had arrived that a large federal army and naval force was en route to Fernandina from Hilton Head Island, South Carolina. On February 19, Brigadier General James H. Trapier sent a letter to General Robert E. Lee, informing him of his concerns that Fernandina was indefensible. On February 24, Lee sent the following letter to Trapier.

Savannah, GA
February 24, 1862

Brigadier General J.H. Trapier
Commanding, &c., Tallahassee,

General, I have the honor to acknowledge the receipt of your letter of
February, from Fernandina, relative to the indefensibility of the position
on Amelia Island. The withdrawal of the troops from Saint Simons and
Jekyll Island can only affect the inland communication between Brunswick
and Cumberland Sound, rendering it less secured and certain. The batteries
commanding the principal entrance into Cumberland Sound can be easily
turned through Saint Andrew's Sound as Saint Simon's, which is nearer
and as accessible as the latter. I had hoped that guns could be obtained in
time to defend theses rear approaches, but as I now see no possibility of
doing so, and as the means on the island are incompetent, in your opinion,
for its defense, you are authorized to retire both from Cumberland and
Amelia Islands to the main land, taking such positions as will best defend
the interests of the state and using the guns and troops for that purpose.
Captain Blain's company must be sent as soon as possible to this city to
report to General Lawton.

The withdrawal of the troops and guns will have to be done with
extreme caution, and your arrangements for that purpose must be done so
quietly and executed so speedily as not to attract the attention of the enemy.
The guns from Cumberland should first be removed and transported across
at night; logs in imitation of guns should be mounted in their places as the
guns are removed. The same precaution should be taken in dismantling the
batteries at Amelia Island; the platforms, ammunition and munitions of
all sorts secured. It is hoped that the guns and ammunition derived from
these points will enable you to secure other important points in the state of
Florida, for supplying which I see no other means.

I am &c,
R.E. Lee
general, commanding[13]

With the enemy possibly only days away, the tasks ahead included the
withdrawal of thirty-three pieces of artillery and munitions of various
sizes and calibers, along with over two thousand troops of infantry,

artillery and cavalry—not to mention Fernandina's civilian population. Colonel Edward Hopkins of the Fourth Regiment Florida Infantry was the commander of Confederate forces at Fernandina and Fort Clinch and took charge of the evacuation. With only a few days to spare, Hopkins put the withdrawal into motion and worked day and night to complete the task of removing the guns and supplies. The work was made difficult, as much of it had to be done at night so as not to draw the attentions of the ever-growing number of U.S. navy warships patrolling the water just offshore of Amelia and Cumberland Islands. The first cannons removed were those on Cumberland Island, and they were followed by the sand and palm log battery just south of Fort Clinch. Next, the Old and New Town Battery cannons were removed, and the New Town cannons were simply put on the train, as the battery was next to the rail line, and the last position at the railroad bridge battery was located four miles away. Of the thirty-three pieces of artillery and the limited time to remove them, nineteen were saved by the Confederate forces.

The Florida Railroad was of great use in assisting the army in its evacuation, as the trains ran day and night. Senator Yulee ensured that the railroad was fully assisting with the evacuation of Fernandina. The railroad workers applied every effort to help the Confederate forces, with the engineers, brakeman, and conductors leaving the trains only for quick visits with family before driving the trains, which were loaded down with troops and supplies, off the island. In addition to the trains, boats, barges and even passenger steamships were used to transport troops and supplies to the mainland of Florida.

Some troops had already left, as was the case of the Twenty-Fourth Mississippi Infantry, which arrived in late November and was the first full regiment to leave by the end of January. They were followed by the remaining troops in a short time. The citizens of Fernandina were not in such a rush, and many citizens waited until the last minute to depart. Over the course of several days, from February 25 to the first arrival of the vanguard of federal warships on February 28, 1862, the citizens took little notice to the warnings that were issued by Colonel Hopkins and other military leaders. Even former senator David L. Yulee was still in town and made his departure on the last train.

On February 27, 1862, the federal navy's vanguard of warships made its appearance in the waterway behind Cumberland Island and at the entrance to the Cumberland Sound. Only the shallow draft vessels were able to navigate the intercoastal waters, so the deep draft ships had to arrive outside

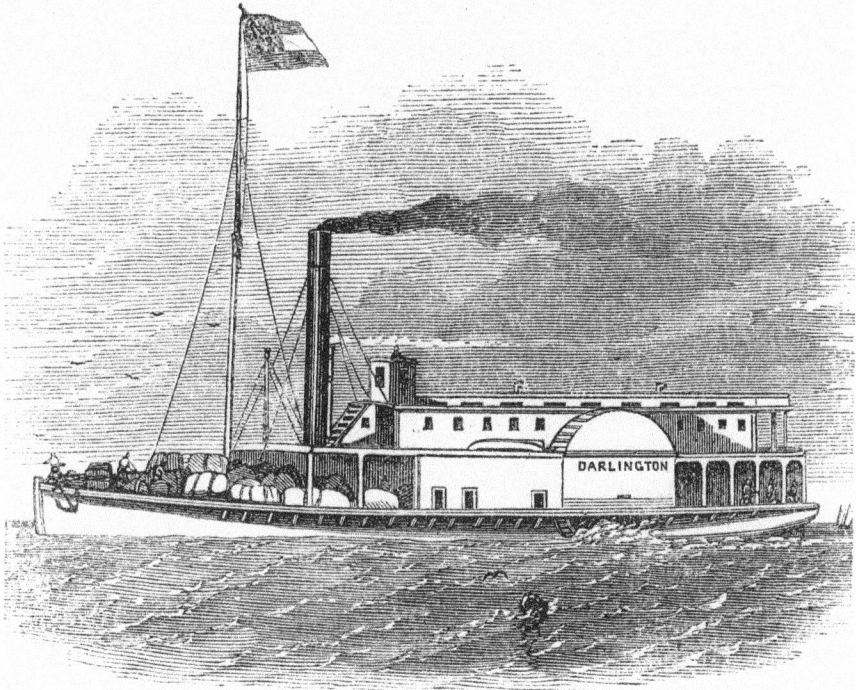

No. 671.—REBEL STEAMER DARLINGTON, CAPTURED IN FERNANDINA HARBOR.

Loaded with Confederate supplies and civilians, the steamship *Darlington* was captured while escaping the federal invasion. *Courtesy of the State Archives of Florida.*

the sound. Once he arrived at his headquarters in Tallahassee, Florida, on February 23, Brigadier General James H. Trapier was ordered to withdraw all Confederate forces from Amelia and Cumberland Islands by order of General Robert E. Lee. General Trapier sent a telegram to Colonel Edward Hopkins, the then-commander of the Confederate forces at Fernandina, to evacuate. After receiving the order on February 25, Colonel Hopkins consulted with Colonel McBlair and discussed the most effective means to withdraw the artillery and troops. This was their greatest challenge, as thirty-three cannons and around 1,500 troops were still posted to Fernandina, along with a civilian population of 1,400. Colonel Hopkins assigned Colonel McBlair and his troops to begin the removal of artillery and made announcements that trains from the Florida Railroad were available to move citizens to the mainland along with any businesses that needed to relocate.

One such business was the Bank of Fernandina, which was chartered in 1859 and dealt with most of the financial transactions of the residents and business owners of Fernandina. The bank was relocated to Stark, Florida, where it continued to operate during the war.

On March 1, 1862, Hopkins directed the Marion Light Artillery, under the command of Captain John Marshall Martin, to take a position on the mainland side of the Amelia River to provide artillery support and to ensure the defense of the evacuating southern forces. Captain Martin was instructed to leave only the men who were necessary to man the field artillery pieces and return to Fernandina with the rest of his men to render assistance. With the artillery in position, the Marion Dragoons, led by Captain William A. Owens, were ordered to do the same. At this critical point in the withdrawal, the residents of Fernandina made little preparation to leave, even after Colonel Hopkins informed the citizens that ample transportation would be furnished to all who desired to leave the island.

The posting of the evacuation information, again, had little effect on the citizens, and on March 2, Hopkins made a second announcement that a special train for women and children would leave the city. The citizens, again, took little interest. That same day, a ship flying a French flag entered the Cumberland Sound and called on the harbor pilot by means of signal flag. Since the ship was a foreign-flagged vessel, Lieutenant Colonel D.P. Holland of the First Florida Battalion, with a detachment of six soldiers from the Fourth Florida Infantry, rowed out to the ship and, on making contact, were taken prisoner, as the ship was a federal navy vessel. It was sometime later that Lieutenant Colonel Holland and the soldiers were released. That same day, additional warships arrived at the Cumberland Sound and in front of Fort Clinch; the total naval presence was not yet learned, as the bulk of the invasion fleet was still on its way. Colonel Hopkins was becoming more concerned, as his position was critical with the enemy warships within sight of his headquarters.

By 6:30 p.m., Hopkins ordered the remaining troops to break camps and forward all needed equipment to the railroad station. This endeavor was not completed until 2:00 a.m. on March 3. Hopkins was informed by courier by Colonel Styles that nineteen to twenty enemy warships had been spotted at Saint Andrews Sound at the north end of Cumberland Island. By 2:30 a.m., the troops who had not already crossed the trestle bridge were ordered to make their way to the mainland. Hopkins retained three companies of the Fourth Florida Infantry to provide protection of Fernandina's citizens, and by sunrise on March 3, the enemy's warships were in full force and view. At

General Robert E. Lee authorized the abandonment of Fernandina and Fort Clinch by Confederate forces. *Courtesy of the State Archives of Florida.*

1:00 p.m., the U.S. Navy started its movement into the Amelia River and advanced on the town. Colonel Hopkins waited with Colonel McBlair to take leave from the town, allowing the trains with citizens and Confederate forces and supplies to evacuate first and allowing the steamboats to depart the docks with passengers and military stores.

The last train pulled away from the railroad depot, carrying citizens, baggage, former senator Yulee, former governor Broome and General Joseph Finegan. The train drew the attention of the warships nearing the docks of Fernandina, and the lead ship hailed the train to stop by firing a warning shot. However, the engineers continued to increase speed, hoping to prevent the capture of the train and its citizens. When the train was about two miles from the trestle bridge, the USS *Ottawa* fired a broadside directly toward the train. As the shots and shells passed and exploded in and around the train, one shell found its mark, scoring a direct hit on the platform car, near the end, which was loaded with furniture. The blast sent the items in all directions, including two young boys named Thompson and Savage, who were killed instantly.

With the damaged train cars and citizens leaping from the train, the engineers were forced to bring the train to a halt, working quickly to disconnect the damaged cars. The train was not in direct view at this point, and the warship was unable to obtain a clear field of fire. Many of the citizens who had leapt from the train were able to make their way to another train that was about a mile ahead and out of range of the warship's cannons. The train made its escape, and once it was over the trestle bridge, Colonel Hopkins gave the order to Second Lieutenant Deakle of the Fourth Regiment Florida Infantry to set fire to the railroad trestle bridge.

Another daring escape was that of the steamship *Darlington*. After the USS *Ottawa* was unsuccessful in stopping and capturing the train, the *Darlington* become its next objective. As the *Darlington* attempted to make its way down the river, the *Ottawa* gave pursuit. The steamship was loaded with women, children, personal baggage, military stores, mules and Dr. H.G. Lungren, the brigade surgeon of the Confederate forces. Captain Brook, the *Darlington*'s skipper, was hoping to escape from the advancing federal navy. Even as the cannons of the *Ottawa* fired on the vessel, with shots landing in the water and shells bursting over the *Darlington*, Captain Brooke held his course and refused to yield or consider surrendering the vessel. The women who were onboard with their children saw that the

To evacuate Confederate forces, the Florida Railroad moved troops and civilians to safety from invading federal forces. *Courtesy of the State Archives of Florida.*

Ottawa was overtaking them and pleaded with the captain to stop. Captain Brooke stopped the vessel, and it, along with its military stores, became the property of the United States, and the southern citizens who were onboard were then in the custody of the U.S. military.

Over the course of the next weeks and months, the Confederate forces of Fernandina and Fort Clinch made their way to Tallahassee, with some troops heading to Pensacola to join the Confederate forces that were assembling there. The Third and Fourth Florida Infantry Regiments would see service in the western theaters of the Civil War, fighting with the Confederate Army of the Tennessee. The Marion Light Artillery would go on to serve with Confederate General E. Kirby Smith and would see action on August 14, 1862, at the Battle of Richmond, Kansas. The Marion Dragoons were considered by General Robert E. Lee to be the finest and most superbly mounted unit when he conducted his tour of inspection in January 1862, and they went on to serve in Florida throughout the war, and they saw service with J.J. Dickerson.

The abandonment of Amelia Island was a great surprise and very difficult for many Confederate officers and men, along with the leadership of the state and the citizens of Fernandina. The massive buildup of artillery batteries, along with the troops assigned to defend the island and its waterways was in the greatest interest of the cause for which they were fighting. However, the reality of the lack of strong defensive positions farther north, along the Georgia coast, and the need for cannon powder, artillery ammunition, small arms and the required musket ammunition brought a turning point in the eyes of the military commanders like General Trapier and, ultimately, General Lee.

For almost fourteen months, Amelia Island, with its Old and New Towns of Fernandina, along with Fort Clinch, was the hustle and bustle of Confederate activity in Northeast Florida. The hope of peace had long vanished, and the reality of war had finally reached this little seaport community. The greatest hardship faced by the residents of Fernandina was the loss of their homes and way of life; they did not know when or if they could return, and that was a hard reality to face. They had hoped to see the island stand up to the enemy and achieve southern independence, which would have allowed them to remain in their homes at Fernandina.

FEDERAL INVASION AND OCCUPATION

With the secession of the southern states from the Union, the United States military lost key forts, arsenals and naval ports throughout the South; the focus of the Union was to regain them, if possible. Brevet Lieutenant General Winfield Scott proposed a naval blockade of the southern coastline known as Scott's Great Snake. Blocking each major seaport would prevent the Confederate states from receiving the materials from foreign nations they were relying on. Even before the first major land battle took place, a meeting was held on July 5, 1861, to discuss the capture and occupation of southern seaports. If the blockade was to be successful, the U.S. Navy needed a southern base to operate from. Officers of the United States military held a council to discuss the importance of securing important seaports along the South Carolina, Georgia and Florida coasts. A report of the findings was sent to the secretary of the navy, Gideon Welles.

Washington, D.C., July 5, 1861
Hon. Gideon Welles
Secretary of the Navy, Washington, D.C.

Sir, We have the honor to inform you that the conference, in compliance with your wishes, communicated through Captain Du Pont, has had under consideration that part of your letter of instructions of the 25th ultimo which relates to the necessity of occupying two or more points on the Atlantic

The Anaconda Plan, a U.S. naval blockade of all southern ports, was referred to as Scotts Great Snake. *Courtesy of the Library of Congress.*

Coast, Fernandina being particularly mentioned as one of these points. It seems to be indispensable that there should exist a convenient coal depot on the southern extremity of the line of Atlantic blockade, and it occurs to the conference that, if this coal depot were suitably selected, it might be used not only as a depot for coal, but as a depot for provisions and common stores, as a harbor of refuge, and as a general rendezvous of headquarters for that part of the coast. We separated in our minds the two enterprises of a purely military expedition and an expedition the principal object of which is the establishment of a naval station for promoting the efficiency of the blocked. We shall have the honor to present plans for both the expeditions. But we will begin with the latter, premising, however, that we think both should be conducted simultaneously.

Fernandina is, by its position, obviously the most suitable point for a place of deposit, answering at one end of the line to Hampton roads at the other. In addition to its position in this respect, it enjoys several other

53

advantages almost peculiar to itself and is well suited to the object in view. It has fourteen feet of water on the bar at low water and twenty at high water, a convenient depth for all steam vessels of the navy, either propelled by screws or side wheels, rated as first-class steam-sloops, which are propelled by screws and by most of the same class propelled by side wheels, when light, and by all the newly purchased and chartered steamers of every description, with the exception, perhaps, of one or two of the very largest mail packet steamers, when deeply loaded. These depths are perfectly convenient for the new sloops and gunboats now on the stocks and for the ordinary merchant vessels chartered for freight. The main ship channel over Saint Marys bar into Fernandina Harbor, though not direct, is by no means tortuous or difficult. It is defined by buoys, and range by means of beacons renders the passage of the bar itself secure. A steam tug will always be at hand to take in sailing vessels when necessary. Inside of the bar, there is an unlimited extent of deep-water accommodation and also the protection of smooth water before reaching the land-locked basins. The anchorage in Amelia River possesses the quiet and safety of an enclosed dock. Repairs of all kinds may be carried on there without the fear of accidents arising from motion of water. The town of Fernandina and the wharves and depots of the Florida Railroad Company furnish conveniences, the value of which need not be enlarged upon. If the seizure were conducted so suddenly as to prevent the destruction of property and building, which it would be difficult to replace, the facilities for landing and storing coal and other materials will be found ready for use. Another feature of this port, and one which has appeared to us to be of sufficient importance to engage your particular attention, is the isolated position of Fernandina, territorially and in population. Fernandina is on an island, bound by the ocean on one side and having on the other an interior poor and uninteresting in all respects, spares in population, remote from large cities or centers of military occupation and not easily accessible by railroad or water communication.

By the census of 1850, the population of Fernandina was about 600; it is now 1,000; Saint Marys, 700; Darian, 500; Jacksonville, 1,145; Saint Augustine, 1,934. The distance by water from Fernandina to Saint Marys is 9 miles; to Brunswick is 35 miles; to Darian is 51 miles. By railroad to Baldwin is 47 miles; from Baldwin to Jacksonville is 20 miles; from Fernandina to Savannah by water is 120 miles; from Fernandina to Charleston is 166 miles; from Fernandina to Cedar Key by railroad is 154 miles, and from Fernandina to Tallahassee by railroad is 192 miles.

With all the above mentioned places, there is water communication, except Cedar Keys, Tallahassee, and the railroad stations between them; but it is apparent that any military opposition of weight must come from Savannah and Charleston, principally through Cumberland Sound, and the depth less than ten feet in some places of this line of interior navigation would require the transportation of the troops in the light steamer employed there. These steamers are so light and devoid of shelter that an expedition would hardly be undertaken if Amelia Island were properly garrisoned. The environs of Fernandina form a natural protection against an attack by land. They consist of marsh and sand, which alone compose the shores of the rivers and bayous.

We are careful to avoid making this communication unnecessarily long by entering upon a comparison of Fernandina with other places in the same region of coast, such as Brunswick, for example, which is now connected by railroad with Savannah, and, being more in the interior, is less healthy; St. John's entrance, which could be fortified against us and has an insuperable objection in its bar; but we take pains to say that such comparisons have formed a large part of our study of the whole subject. We have not spoken of the peculiar advantages of Fernandina as a depot and naval station without attaching a meaning to the word. Although an open and rapid communication with the Gulf of Mexico by the Florida Railroad to Cedar Keys accomplished in eleven hours would undoubtedly be desirable, still it has not entered into our project to recommend the maintenance of this communication. To do so would employ a force disproportionate to the possible benefits to be derived from it. The central railroad to Tallahassee, which connects with this road at Baldwin, is completed as far as Alligator, and for a certain distance from Tallahassee east about twenty miles. The country on the line of the road is thickly wooded and has few inhabitants. A road of such length 154 miles, in an obscure and inhospitable district, may be easily rendered impassable. Fort Clinch is not thought to be defensible in its present condition, and the sand batteries on the shore can probably be easily turned. The water is so smooth in ordinary times on the outer shore of Amelia that a landing can be affected there with facility and will, in our opinion, be advisable at more than one point. This landing cannot be covered by large ships, especially such as the screw frigates. Vessels of small draft must be selected for this duty, and when the points of landing are fixed upon, the line of approach for the covering vessels must be distinctly traced out. The Florida Railroad, from the west shoe of Amelia Island across the river, is built on piles for the distance of about one mile, similar to the long bridge across the Bush and Gun Powder. When the attack is made, one or more small gunboats might take the back entrance, through Nassau Inlet and Sound, and prevent the destruction of this bridge by the rebels. Nassau's entrance is no doubt unguarded. Nassau Bar has only five feet of water on it, and even this depth is not to be relied upon. Launches may therefore be employed. A rapid survey, immediately preceding the attack, will correct any misapprehension on this point. The preservation of this trestle bridge is worth an effort. The remainder of the road can be replaced with less cost, because it runs through a naturally level country. It is estimated that 3,000 men could take and hold the place, with the assistance of such forces as could be furnished by the fleet. After the place was taken, a portion of the defensive force would be found on board the vessels in port. Thus, the number of troops to be added to the marines and seamen employed in the attack and subsequent defense would not, probably at any time, exceed the number of 3,000.

The details of the expedition to Fernandina, if decided upon, will fall under the several bureaus of the war and navy departments and the chefs of the expedition, to whom the conference will be always ready to offer such information and make such suggestions as may result from their careful study of the ground. The sailing directions for the Port of Fernandina, the instructions for the disposition of the buoys and beacons, the outer and inner anchorages, the pilotage and the meteorology of this section of the coast will hereafter be furnished by the conference from the archives of the coast survey. It is known that Fernandina is healthy and that it can supply wood and water in abundance. Its market supplies remain to be developed. Finally, we will repeat the remark made in the beginning of this report, that we think the expedition to Fernandina should be undertaken simultaneously with a similar expedition having a purely military character. We are preparing a brief report on the latter, which we shall have the honor to submit in a few days.

We have the honor to be, most respectfully, your obedient servants,
S.F. Dupont Captain U.S. Navy, President.
J.G. Barnard, Major, U.S. Engineers, Member.
A.D. Bache, Superintendent, U.S. Coast Survey, Member.
Chas. H. Davis, Commander, U.S. Navy, Member and Secretary.[14]

In October 1861, a joint military force of the army and navy commanded by Brigadier General Thomas W. Sherman and Admiral Samuel F. Du Pont assembled at Hampton Roads, Virginia, with a naval force of seventy-seven

A federal expeditionary force assembled in 1861 to capture coastal South Carolina, Georgia and Florida. It was comprised of seventy-seven ships and thirteen thousand troops. *Courtesy of the Library of Congress.*

ships carrying thirteen thousand troops. The force was used in the expedition against the South Carolina, Georgia and Florida coasts.

The orders called for the navy to transport the army and capture the area south of Charleston, South Carolina, mainly Port Royal, Beaufort and Hilton Head Island. The orders were carried out between November 3 and November 7, 1861. With the capture and occupation of these points, the next stage of military operations was to capture and occupy Amelia Island, Florida, along with its seaport towns of Old and New Fernandina and Fort Clinch. The army forces under the command of General T.W. Sherman were divided into three separate infantry brigades. General Horatio G. Wright commanded the Third Brigade Expeditionary Force and was ordered to proceed south with Admiral Du Pont's naval forces to capture Fernandina. The naval forces consisted of twenty-eight ships, with a portion of the flotilla made up of several shallow draft vessels that could traverse the narrow and shallow waterways around Cumberland and Amelia Islands. Several ships comprised the vanguard of the fleet proceeding south on the afternoon of February 27, and the remaining fleet left on the morning of February 28, 1862. The ships were placed in the following order as they entered the Saint Andrew's Sound, north of Cumberland Island, and proceeded into the waterway behind Cumberland Island. First came the USS *Ottawa*, followed by the *Mohican, Seminole, Pawnee, Pocahontas, Flag, Florida, James Adger, Bienville, Alabama, Keystone State, Seneca, Huron, Pembina, Isaac Smith, Penguin, Potomska* and *McClellan*. The remaining ships, including USS *Wabash, Pilot Boat Hope, Revenue Cutter Henrietta, Star of the South, Belvedere, Empire City, Boston, Cosmopolitan, Onward* and *Susquehanna*, headed down the coast by way of the

Atlantic Ocean. Also traveling with the fleet were the schooners *Sarah Cullen, Marion, J.G. Steele, R.J. Mercer, Susan F. Abbott, George's Creek, Blackbird* and *Ellen,* carrying various military supplies and provisions.

As the fleet arrived in the main shipping channel of the Cumberland Sound, in front of Fort Clinch and the inland waterway, the fleet dropped anchor and remained in place until the afternoon of March 3, 1862. Onboard the flagship, which arrived on March 2, an African American fisherman gladly reported to Admiral Du Pont and General Wright that Confederate forces were in the process of abandoning Fernandina. The news of the enemy's withdrawal was considered, and the commanders made the decision to invade on March 3. The orders were relayed to the commanders of the other ships, along with the army's regimental commanders. The army forces involved were the Fourth New Hampshire Infantry Regiment, Ninth Maine Infantry Regiment, Ninety-Seventh Pennsylvania Infantry Regiment, two companies of the First Regiment New York Volunteer Engineers, Company C and E, Battery E, Third United States Artillery and Major Reynold's United States Marine Battalion. The combined forces of the army and marines totaled approximately 3,663 officers and men.

Just after 1:00 p.m., the invasion commenced, with sailors and marines from the USS *Wabash* and the USS *Ottawa*, commanded by Lieutenant G.M. White, landing on the eastern front of Fort Clinch and proceeding along the glacis, where they entered the sally port on the southwest front of the fort. In the vanguard of the leading force, the marines found the area deserted of all persons. They proceeded to make a full tour of the fort, where Lieutenant White noticed the flagpole lying on the parade field along with construction materials and three large-caliber cannons. The sailors brought forward ship axes and made quick work of shortening the pole for movement to the top of the north bastion. Once it was anchored in place, the detachment proceeded to raise the stars and stripes with a jubilant cheer. The sailors and army troops still aboard the ships also noticed the raising of the flag. Fort Clinch was returned to the Union. The raising of the flag made Fort Clinch the first third-system fortification returned to the control of the United States. As the warships proceeded into the Amelia River, the *Ottawa, Mohican* and *Huron* were followed by transport vessels, which held sailors and army forces to be landed at Old Town Fernandina and, eventually, New Town.

The purpose of the advancing warships was twofold: to capture any enemy forces and to stop the destruction of public and private property by the enemy. As the last train pulled away from the railroad depot, the USS *Ottawa* gave chase along the Amelia River. It was determined that the train

Brigadier General Thomas W. Sherman commanded the army during the expedition to the South Carolina, Georgia and Florida coasts. *Courtesy of the Library of Congress.*

carried Confederate forces or some small portion of them because, from the window of the coach and platform cars, the Southern soldiers made several attempts to fire at the *Ottawa* from the moving train. Onboard the warship, the commander, Captain Stevens, attempted to hail the train to stop without success and ordered the gun crew to engage the train. The *Ottawa* was an Unadilla-class warship, which is also referred to as a ninety-day gunboat; it was armed with an eleven-inch shell gun and twenty-four pounder cannons. The ship began firing on the train, and several rounds came close to scoring a hit. One shot flew right over the train engineers' smokestack and others fell beside the cars. Just a short distance from the railroad trestle, the *Ottawa* gunners found their range when a bursting shell exploded on the platform car near the end of the train. The explosion blasted through furniture and supplies and instantly killed two sixteen-year-old boys, John M. Thompson and M. Savage. The young boys were decimated by the explosion, as the federal soldiers observed a day later; the event was recalled by Brigade Quartermaster Captain Goodrich.

> *I went up to the depot and saw the car and sofa that the two men were killed on. The sofa was covered with blood and brains. On a table lay a piece of jaw and a mass of scalp with the hair on it. The car was a complete wreck.* [15]

A few days later, Savage's brother sought the assistance of the federal army to collect the remains of the two boys for burial. Dr. Craven, a military surgeon, assisted Savage's brother by providing a cart to collect their remains and convey the bodies to the town cemetery.

The Ninth Regiment Maine Infantry was the first to land at New Town Fernandina, and it established advance picket forces with reconnaissance conducted by the Ninth Maine and supported by the Ninety-Seventh Pennsylvania Infantry, which made its landing at Old Town Fernandina. Due to the size of Amelia Island (thirteen miles long and one mile wide), the infantry forces completely scouted the island to ensure there were no remaining Confederate forces, and companies of the Ninth Maine conducted roving patrols to prevent looting. The Fourth New Hampshire Infantry Regiment also put ashore, with a few companies assigned to Fort Clinch and the connecting military road to Old Fernandina. At the lighthouse, the federal forces discovered that the navigation lens had been taken by the retreating Confederates; because of this, a lookout station with the ability to signal ships entering the main channel was established.

Over the next few days, the establishment of quarters, camps and security around Amelia Island was a priority. A rumor began that the Confederates were planning their return; however, this was not the case. Since the burning of the railroad trestle bridge, trains or troops were unable to cross the Amelia River, and the navy secured the Amelia River with its warships. With the trestle bridge still burning, Lieutenant Downes and a detachment of sailors from the USS *Huron* attempted to extinguish the fire and salvage the bridge; however, the main supports were damaged beyond saving. The railroad on the island was in a good state, as two locomotives, boxcars, tenders and freight cars were discovered.

The capture of Fernandina and Fort Clinch was deemed a great success. The federal forces captured fifteen pieces of artillery that were abandoned by the retreating Confederates, along with other valuable stores and provisions. To oversee the command of the Union forces, army headquarters were set up at the home of former senator David L. Yulee. Former governor Broome's home was also occupied by the paymaster, Major Pangborn of the U.S. Volunteers and the Signal Corps. The post hospital was housed in Confederate colonel Dale's home, and Confederate general Finnegan's home was occupied by Colonel Rich, the regimental commander of the Ninth Maine. Other evacuated homes and buildings, especially those along the waterfront, were set up to receive supplies to maintain the federal forces. Many empty homes were used as officers' quarters, while some troops were

Right: Commanding the Third Brigade to capture Fernandina, Fort Clinch, Brigadier General Horatio G. Wright was successful on March 3, 1861, with the capture of Amelia Island. *Courtesy of the Library of Congress.*

Below: Three successful landings were made by federal forces to capture Fernandina and Fort Clinch. *Courtesy of the State Archives of Florida.*

THE WAR IN FLORIDA—OLD FERNANDINA, AMELIA ISLAND, LOOKING N. E., SHOWING THE OLD SPANISH EARTHWORKS.—FROM A SKETCH BY OUR SPECIAL RTIST ATTACHED TO COM. DUPONT'S EXPEDITION.—SEE PAGE 382.

quartered in camps and others were quartered at the First Presbyterian and Saint Peter's Episcopal Churches. The citizens who remained were required to register at the provost office, and a curfew was put in place, restricting citizens from going out past 8:00 p.m. The towns, both old and new, were surrounded by federal troops, with the navy controlling the waterway and associated piers and docks.

At Fort Clinch, Captain Alfred F. Sears was placed in command by general orders of the war department, and a special order came from the chief of the army's corps of engineers, Brigadier Joseph G. Totten, to resume the fort's construction. Two companies of the First New York Volunteer Engineer Regiment were then serving; Company C served at the fort, and Company E served in Old Town Fernandina. General Horatio G. Wright, the first federal commander of Fernandina Post, prepared to leave with the navy and a battalion of the Fourth New Hampshire, the Ninety-Seventh Pennsylvania Infantry Regiments and Battery E Third U.S. Artillery to occupy Jacksonville, Florida. The Ninth Maine Regiment remained at Fernandina and Fort Clinch along with three companies of the Fourth New Hampshire. A combined force of two companies of New York Engineers had about 1,500 federal solders. The invasion of Amelia Island had been a bloodless effort for the federal forces.

To ensure the security of their newly acquired position, the federal forces set up picket lines around Old and New Town, with an advance picket post located one mile in front of Fort Clinch. The picket posts were created to maintain control over the movement of soldiers and civilians, and only those with passes were permitted to leave the towns. A roving patrol was responsible for traveling around Amelia Island on horseback to maintain a more advanced picket position; the army established watch points on the south end of the island. A company of troops was established on nearby Piney Island, close to the railroad trestle bridge that connected the island to the mainland. A watch station was placed on Cumberland Island to monitor any enemy ships that may have attempted to leave by way of the Saint Marys River.

On April 10, 1862, the advanced picket post on Piney Island, also known as Judge O'Neal's place, was attacked by Confederate forces in the early morning hours.

Report of Lieut. Col. H. Bisbee Jr., Ninth Maine Infantry
Headquarters
Fernandina, FL, April 27, 1862

Report in case of a party of men belonging to Company 1, Ninth Maine Regiment, captured by the enemy on the 10th of April 1862. Names of the party: Orderly Sergt. Richard Webster, Corp. James W. Bowman, Private Isaac Whitney, John E. Kent, Alonzo B. Merrill, C. Wesley Adams, taken prisoners; private Ansel Chase, killed.

At the time the above party were captured and killed, Company 1 was doing picket duty at the railroad bridge, which span's the creek separating Amelia Island from the mainland. They were captured at what is known in this vicinity as the Judge O'Neal's Place, which is about two miles and a half from the railroad bridge. The captain of the company S.D. Baker allowed this party of men on the 7th of April to remain at said Judge O'Neal's place to protect the wife of one Mr. Heath, whom I held in arrest at the time, and who was living at O'Neal's house. Captain Baker left the party at said place without reporting it to his commanding officer, doing it as an act of kindness and sympathy for Mrs. Heath, and as his men daily frequented the vicinity with impunity and did not think that he was doing a wrong act of exposing his men. On the same day, 7th of April, Private William W. Lunt of Company I, Ninth Maine Regiment, deserted, went to the enemy's lines, and it is supposed, reported to the enemy that this party of men was stationed at Judge O'Neal's. On Thursday, 10th of April, Captain Baker sent two men to order the party in, who found the dead body of one man that, from appearances, had been shot that day, and the remainder of the party taken prisoners.

Very respectfully,
H. Bisbee Jr.,
Lieutenant Colonel Ninth Maine Regiment[16]

Throughout 1862, federal forces participated in several small expeditions around Amelia Island and made several trips up the Saint Marys River; they brought back captured supplies and contraband, which greatly affected the Confederate forces in the area. Civilians from the North began arriving with government contracts in hand to provide for the navy and army. The commander was concerned with sutlers selling goods, and he feared that alcohol would find its way into the hands of the troops. Although alcohol was prohibited, it found its way into the hands of the troops garrisoning the towns. To combat the problem of alcohol sales, the provost ordered inspections of the sutler tents and shops two to three times a week, and all merchant ships were inspected jointly with the navy. During one inspection, it was discovered that a sutler who was selling goods from his schooner was responsible for the sale of alcohol to soldiers. When the provost found the strong brew, he had its barrel head broken, and it was poured into the river. Witnesses said the alcohol was so powerful that it astonished the fish.

The army used the trains located at the docks of New Fernandina to move troops and supplies weekly to the defensive position at the railroad bridge. While the Confederates were concerned about a federal assault from sea, the federal troops were concerned about a Confederate assault from

Federal troops conducted a grand parade to celebrate the successful invasion and capture of Fernandina. *Courtesy of the State Archives of Florida.*

the mainland. To safeguard the vital towns and the waterfront, the army constructed new artillery battery positions and improved those that were abandoned by the enemy. At Old Town, in the former location of Fort San Carlos, the federals installed two thirty-two-pound cannons at the northern end of New Town on a high bluff, a position that was established with two twenty-four-pounders. They also installed two thirty-two-pounders and one captured eight-inch mortar at the railroad bridge.

In 1863, Battery Plaisted was built in the marsh between Old and New Town. For the troops assigned there, it was miserable during the summers, with the mosquitos and flies, and in the fall and winter, the wet, cold weather crept into their bones, as one soldier stated. With the island secured, the navy began making major improvements to the piers and docks of New Town, including enlarging the coaling station and building cisterns to provide drinking water for the fleet. Blacksmith shops, sail shops and carpenter workshops were also built to repair navy vessels. The train tracks were extended farther north, to the end of the piers, and new warehouses and living quarters were built for the sailors and marines. It was a massive undertaking; however, it was what the July 5, 1861 report was looking to accomplish after Fernandina was captured by the Union. Fernandina maintained the navy's ability to block the southern coast from Hampton Roads, Virginia, to Key West. Through the rest of 1862, the navy's efforts

One thousand citizens evacuated Fernandina before the federal invasion; four hundred stayed behind. *Courtesy of the State Archives of Florida.*

to improve the Port of Fernandina was a great success, and in the post–Civil War years, the town benefitted from the work the navy had completed during the war.

A large local mansion was used to provide medical care for the federal forces. The first floor received the sick and injured soldiers, sailors and marines; the second floor served as a hospital ward; and the third floor was used for surgeries. A catwalk connected the mansion to a house directly behind it, where meals were prepared and supplies were stored. A small house next to the mansion served as quarters for the military doctors (surgeons) and the medical staff, which included the regimental hospital stewards. Ladies with the sanitary commission assisted with the town's medical needs and helped the medical corps acquire the necessary supplies to care for troops and the civilians of Fernandina. With the evacuation of Southern forces, many residents of Fernandina lost their doctors, which left the medical needs of the citizens who remained to the federal army. During the occupation, five army surgeons and two contracted civilian doctors from the North served as caregivers, along with a contracted dentist who one soldier claimed was quite efficient at pulling teeth.

The following federal army regiments, battalions and companies served at Fernandina Post and Fort Clinch from March 1862 to December 1862: the Ninth Maine Infantry Regiment; three companies of the Fourth New Hampshire; along with Companies C and E of the First New York Engineers. The troops were placed at the following locations: Companies B, H and K of the Fourth New Hampshire were located at New Town; Company C of the First New York Engineers were assigned to Fort Clinch; Company E was stationed at Old Fernandina; and the Ninth Maine was divided between Fort Clinch, Old Town, the railroad bridge battery and at the southern end of Amelia Island. Colonel Rishworth Rich of the Ninth Maine served as the commander of Fernandina Post from March 19, 1862, to December 31, 1862, after replacing General Wright.

To maintain proficiency in the soldier drills, the troops followed a regimented schedule of duties referred to the general calls of the day. These calls provided the soldiers with signaling for assigned duties, and meal breaks were sounded by the bugle, fife and drum. reveille was at daybreak, breakfast was at 7:00 a.m., surgeons' call was at 7:30 a.m., guard mounting was at 8:00 a.m., dinner was at 12:00 p.m., police call was at 6:30 a.m. and 5:00 p.m., dress parade was at sunset, supper was immediately after parade, tattoo was at 8:30 p.m. and taps was played at 9:00 p.m. Daily company drill lasted one hour and commenced at 8:30 a.m., except on Sunday, when it consisted of school of the soldier and infantry tactics, which generally covered soldier formation, drilling in marching and movement, rifle instruction, manual of arms, bayonet drill, platoon and squad drills.

Company commanders and battalion commanders conducted both instruction in the company exercises and battalion drills, along with learning the general upkeep of the soldier equipment and camp gear. In addition to all the training, soldiers were selected and posted to various tasks consistent with guard duty, stable duty, work details and military expeditions to the mainland. All troops received artillery instruction on how to man the batteries, should it be required. The soldiers were required to bathe twice weekly and wash their face, hands and brush their teeth daily. The fife and drummer were also schooled in the calls of the day

With concern over an attack from the mainland, the federal forces strengthened and built batteries facing the river. *Courtesy of the Library of Congress.*

and were assigned to the regiment headquarters and post headquarters to sound necessary calls of the day. Daily officers' meetings were held to review the needed duties of the post with changes in the placement of troops and picket posting about the island.

Captain Sears, the fort's commander, had a different arrangement for his engineering soldiers. The infantry assigned to the fort generally followed Sears's call and, instead of focusing on the construction assignments, the infantry carried out school of the soldier instruction, artillery drill and guard duty. This, in many cases, relieved the engineers from guard duty and allowed them to continue the fort's construction. Captain Sears sounded the following calls at Fort Clinch: reveille at daybreak, assembly at 6:00 a.m., fatigue call at 6:30 a.m., breakfast at 7:00 a.m., work call, stable call, sergeant's at call 7:30 a.m., dinner call at 12:30 p.m., work call at 1:00 p.m., police call at 5:00 p.m., supper call at 5:30 p.m., tattoo at 8:00 p.m. and taps at 8:30 p.m. Captain Sears ordered dress parade to take place weekly on Saturday mornings. A monthly inspection was conducted on the third Wednesday of each month for the engineers, and artillery drills commenced twice every month.

However busy their duties kept them, the soldiers still found time to enjoy the island (even though many wrote of boredom over the course of the federal occupation). A soldier's typical day in Fernandina was sometimes much different from the days of those stationed at Fort Clinch. To entertain the troops, several social groups were formed, including the Visiting Ladies Society from the North, the Christian Commission, the Ladies Sewing Society and the Women's Relief Society, a sanitary commission with female educators. The societies were run by ladies and overseen by male civilians and army commanders in order to prevent the ladies from ending up in situations that would have caused embarrassment. Orders were published forbidding ladies from entering the barracks, camps and quarters of the troops, and they could only enter the fort with an escort and approval of the commanders, as all involvement by women was closely supervised. Prostitution was a constant problem for the army and navy, and it was not regarded as beneficial to the troops; however, brothels were operated throughout the war in Fernandina. Periods of off-duty time were limited, and the soldiers normally spent that time napping; writing and reading letters; reading newspapers; playing card games, athletic games, horseshoes and, of course, rounders, the early form of baseball; and shell collecting, which was a favorite, along with the perpetuating practical joking among comrades.

The arrival of the army paymaster was always a welcome sight, as the officers and enlisted men were meant to be paid monthly by the army. Due to the size and vastness of the Department of the South, the paymasters did not always show up as expected. Although, when he did arrive, all of the back pay was paid to the men. The pay was important to the troops, as it allowed them to purchase the items they needed and to send money home.

While the army was stationed at Fernandina, the health of the army and the fort was of great concern to the medical corps. Soldiers from the North were adjusting to the humid Florida weather, and the intense, oppressive sun caused heat-related illnesses. This was all coupled with the common cold, yellow fever, smallpox and diarrhea. However, the army stationed there did far better than the armies in the fields of Virginia and Tennessee, and although there was sickness in Fernandina during the federal occupation,

To care for federal soldiers and civilians, the army established the post military hospital of Fernandina. *Courtesy of the Library of Congress.*

the death rate was very low. The bodies of those who died were sent home, and those that were not claimed or were unable to be sent home were buried in the town cemetery, Bosque Bello. In 1926, the United States government funded a project in which the remains of federal soldiers who died during the Civil War at Fernandina were moved to the National Cemetery in Beaufort, South Carolina.

The year 1863 saw several extended federal military excursions up the Saint Marys River from Fort Clinch and Fernandina, and in early January, the lumber expedition was launched. Sailing from Hilton Head, South Carolina, the federal forces arrived at Fort Clinch on January 5. Once they were there, the troops received additional supplies and rations for movement upriver. The force was made up of the two companies of the Third New Hampshire Infantry, along with three companies of the Third Rhode Island Heavy Artillery that served as infantry, and the navy provided transportation and armed escort ships. The troops' objective was to destroy the sawmills that were located inland from Fernandina.

However, great plans do not always work out, and by the time the small fleet arrived and the troops landed, the Confederate forces set fire to the lumber stores, and the lumber piles were burned to the ground. Unable to obtain the lumber, the federal forces returned to Fernandina, although it was not the end of the federal operation.

After leaving Hilton Head Island, South Carolina, a new operation was planned that involved one of the first all–African American regiments. The First South Carolina began organizing in May 1862 by recruiting former slaves under the direction of Sergeant Trowbridge. The unit was tasked with a major federal excursion up the Saint Marys River two weeks after the failed lumber expedition. Thomas Wentworth Higginson was offered the command, as he had already raised a white company of Massachusetts men and was then serving as captain of the Fifty-First Massachusetts Infantry Regiment. Higginson was sent to Hilton Head and Beaufort, South Carolina, to observe colored soldiers in training, and after a review and reflection of the offer, Higginson became colonel of the First South Carolina and immediately led the regiment into full service.

The Department of the South's headquarters decided to conduct a federal military operation up the Saint Marys River to capture or destroy supplies that were supporting the local Confederate cause. This included the brickyard, which provided bricks to Fort Clinch before the war; at that time, bricks were important for the fort's completion, along with a large lumber supply stores. Nearly thirty miles upriver, the First South Carolina and its navy escort had to travel to complete the mission. Their success greatly depended on the conduct and character of the new colored troops during their first operation. On January 25, 1863, the First South Carolina arrived at Fort Clinch aboard the ships *John Adams*, *Planter* and *Ben De Ford*; the force was made up of 462 officers and men. After a quick resupply, the battalion ascended the Saint Marys River by ship and was deposited at the desired landing spot just south of Township, Florida. With 100 men and an advance guard, the expedition began after midnight as they came upon the village of Township, where they encircled the village to prevent the citizens from informing the Confederates that federal forces were in the area. However, the enemy was traveling along the same road, and with the advance guard coming to a halt, the sound of cavalry could be heard in the distance. The advance guard fired on the Confederate cavalry, and the two forces exchanged rifle and pistol fire.

With this engagement, the First South Carolina received its baptism in combat, and the men proved themselves to be great soldiers, as many believed they would. The small engagement proved that African American men were willing and able to fight for the preservation of the Union and their long-sought freedom. The expedition resulted in the death of one soldier, seven wounded and an eighth who was unable to recover from his wounds. The Confederates' casualties were reported as twelve killed, including Lieutenant John D. Jones. Colonel Higginson ordered his soldiers to destroy any supplies or property that could be used to aid the enemy, and all of the picket posts they maintained were burned or destroyed. In the process of carrying out his orders, a piano was taken as a prize and given to the Colored Children's School in Fernandina. The engagement became known as the Battle of the Hundred Pines since it was fought in the pine barrens of North Florida.

With news of this success, the First South Carolina once again ascended the Saint Marys River to capture viable lumber and secure bricks for Fort Clinch that it was unable to secure in the first operation. Unlike the previous journey, this one was tedious. At several positions along the banks of the river, the Confederate Home Guard, which was supported by some regular troops, harassed the federal colored troops and the ships they were on. When they reached the landing, the men of the First South Carolina formed two advance guards, with the remaining troops in column formation, and they went about their duties with little assault from the Southern forces. Once they were able to locate the brick yard, the First South Carolina secured forty thousand bricks to deliver to Captain Sears at Fort Clinch. They also took possession of forty bushels of rice, thirty sheep, lumber tools, farming implements, railroad track irons, one thousand feet of lumber and six male prisoners. The ships were so packed that space was limited for soldiers; although they did manage to bring back several African American families. The captured items were delivered to Fernandina, and some items were taken to Hilton Head, South Carolina.

After demonstrating their readiness to defend the Union and fight for their rights to become citizens, the First South Carolina opened the door for thousands of African American men to answer the call to defend and maintain the Union. By the summer of 1863, the ability of the federal forces to move inland, harass the enemy and find those persons who were seeking federal protection was nearly unstoppable. As the population of former slaves in Fernandina grew, their needs fell to the federal army, which aided them and offered them opportunities for paid work. Many African American men found jobs in the Army Quartermaster Corps and Commissary Corps, and others worked for the navy, supporting the ships of the South Atlantic Fleet. At Fort Clinch, Captain Sears employed African American laborers in

Fort Clinch was the first United States fort returned to federal control after being abandoned by the Confederates on March 3, 1862. *Courtesy of the State Archives of Florida.*

the fort's construction and in handling the equipment and supplies that were arriving at the fort's piers. The Delany family was one of the most notable colored families, and they were employed as civilian brick masons. African American workers were paid a wage of ten to seventy-five cents daily, along with rations.

The women who were interviewed by the Council of Administration were offered the opportunity to work as company washwomen or laundresses and were hired by the soldiers for one dollar monthly to wash their uniforms; two to four women employed by each company. Some of the women who were serving as laundresses at Fort Clinch and at the post hospital in town were Louisa Hagan, Diana Kingsley and Jane Mitchell. Located just outside the fort, a tent and, later, a shed were utilized by the washwomen. Each washwoman received one ration daily and were limited to working only during daylight hours two to three days a week.

A tour of inspection that was conducted in December 1863 evaluated the defensive positions of Fernandina and Fort Clinch, including the following list of redoubts and batteries at Fernandina. Fort Clinch was listed as good but unfinished; it defended the approach from the ocean to the Amelia River, Cumberland River and Cumberland Sound. The types and quantities of guns at Fort Clinch included seven twenty-four-pounder siege guns, ten thirty-two-pounder siege guns, three eight-inch Columbiads, eight twenty-four-pounder howitzers flank defense and one six-inch rifle (rebel cannon). Battery Plaisted, which was located in Fernandina, defended the land approach and had two twenty-four-pounder siege guns. Battery Rich, which was in excellent condition and located in Fernandina, defended the west side of the river with one twenty-four-pounder siege gun. The railroad bridge battery, which was in excellent condition and located the near trestle bridge on the west side of Amelia Island had two thirty-two-pounders one eight-inch mortar. In addition to the permanent cannon positions, two ten-pounder parrot rifles were assigned to Fernandina, and a ten-pounder parrot gun and twenty-four-pounder field howitzer were located at Fort Clinch.

From January 1863 to December 1863, the following federal infantry regiments, battalions and companies served at Old and New Town Fernandina and Fort Clinch. The Seventh Connecticut Infantry Regiment served from January 1863 to May 1863. The First New York Engineers, Company E, served at Fort Clinch, and Company C was transferred to Beaufort, South Carolina, in February 1863. The Ninth Maine Infantry was relieved by the Seventh Connecticut, and one company of the Ninth Maine remained there until April 1863. The First South Carolina Infantry went on

Federal forces moved fifteen captured cannons to Fort Clinch and other new batteries that were under construction. *Courtesy of the collection of Clive Powell.*

two expeditions up the Saint Marys River between January and February 1863. In May 1863, the Seventh New Hampshire Infantry Regiment was transferred from Saint Augustine to Fernandina to relieve the Seventh Connecticut. The Seventh New Hampshire served on Amelia Island until June 1863. The Eleventh Maine Infantry Regiment relieved the Seventh New Hampshire and served until October 1863, when they were replaced by the returning Ninety-Seventh Pennsylvania Infantry Regiment. The Fourth United States Colored Troops arrived in July 1863 and continued to serve at both Amelia Island and Cumberland Island until January 1864. The Third New Hampshire Infantry, along with a battalion of the Third Rhode Island Heavy Artillery, was stationed at Fernandina in January 1863, when companies of the regiment and battalion conducted an expedition in the western part of Nassau County.

To oversee the supply of food that was needed to feed the large number of federal forces serving on Amelia Island and the civilian population, the U.S. Quartermaster Corps, along with the Commissary Corps, maintained a steady income of dry goods, fresh vegetables and fruit and two animal stockades. Merchant ships loaded with food stores and other necessary substances arrived weekly. Near the southern end of the pier, just south of the railroad depot, there was a large slaughter yard that consisted of five hundred head of cattle and three hundred hogs that were used to feed the troops and civilians.

The town's daily rations consisted of beef three times a week, pork three times a week and fish once a week. Potatoes, carrots and onions were the most common vegetables, and corn and yams were issued when they were available. The availability of fruit depended on what was in season up north and in the Caribbean. Dry goods of beans, rice, coffee, sugar, salt and pepper were provided along with desiccated or dried vegetables, fruit, flour, yeast, corn meal, oatmeal and vinegar.

The rations we receive are fair to good. We have beef three times a week and pork the rest. Our company cooks, which were selected by the vote of the men, take charge of the rations and go about cooking. Generally speaking, we have biscuits, bacon, and coffee each morning since arriving here and with a stew of pork, potatoes and onions along with biscuits again for dinner.
—Edward Miller, Company E, First New York Engineers[17]

Supper was of beef, onions and rice, along with sweet bread a grand treat.
—Frances Norman, 157th New York[18]

The federal forces occupying the towns turned churches, homes and stores into living quarters, kitchens and bakeries. *Courtesy of the State Archives of Florida.*

In 1863, Mr. Gustavus Stark arrived in Fernandina to open a bakery, where he sold baked goods to civilians and to the army under contract. At Fort Clinch, with the completion of the kitchen and bakery, the troops were able to prepare meals for the garrison. Common fort meals were breakfasts of bacon, biscuits, apple butter or molasses, coffee with sugar and oatmeal; these were followed by dinners of pork or beef with rice or beans and a supper of pork or beef with potatoes and onions. Chickens were scarce after the first year of occupation, as the soldiers had consumed them so quickly. While local fish were readily available, they were not easily obtained, as the soldiers were often too busy to fish. Some soldiers were assigned to the bakery, where they made bread, biscuits, gingerbread cookies, pies and Johnnycake. Common beverages at the fort consisted of coffee for all three meals, bug juice (a punch made with fruits and sugar water), hot tea, water, cider and lime or lemon juice drinks; milk was not available, as the dairy cows were put to slaughter. Special drinks purchased from the sutler were birch beer, ginger beer and cream soda. Overall, the federal forces ate far better than the troops who were in the field or campaigning, and there were few complaints about the food rations at Fernandina or the fort during the war.

The cooks of our mess have oatmeal ready each cold morning; the only thing in the oatmeal is oats and meal. Sometimes they put in raisins, which are just flies without their wings.
—*Levi Rury, Company E, First New York Engineers*[19]

As 1864 began, the federal occupation of Fernandina and Fort Clinch brought in the new year with a grand cotillion for the officers and men. The event offered athletic games; shooting matches; rowboat, horse and wheelbarrow races; religious services; and performances from the regimental band. The navy hosted a firework show over the Amelia River, and an artillery salute was conducted with hopes that the war would end in the new year. The presidential election was taking place that November, and the political debates were already starting to heat up. That year saw a growth in Fernandina's civilian population, and additional schools were opened to educate both white and colored children. The Ninety-Seventh Pennsylvania returned to Fernandina and was posted to locations throughout the island. Company A and G were assigned to Fort Clinch; Company C and the provost guard were assigned to New Town Fernandina; Company E was assigned to the railroad bridge battery; Company H was assigned to Old

To maintain security of Amelia Island, the federal forces posted guard positions around the towns and waterfront. *Courtesy of the Library of Congress.*

Town Fernandina; and the remaining troops were quartered in New Town and camped near Former governor Broome's house. The Twenty-First United States Colored Troops opened a recruiting opportunity for men of color to serve in the federal army; this resulted in 102 African American men joining at Fernandina to serve in the Twenty-First USCT.

On February 14, 1864, a federal expedition headed to King's Ferry in the western part of the county, near the Saint Marys River, from Fernandina. The forces consisted of the 3rd Rhode Island Heavy Artillery, which had two field guns; several companies of the 97th Pennsylvania Infantry; and one company of the 115th New York Infantry. Rumors and collected intelligence suggested the enemy was using the area's ferry to move cattle and other supplies that were used to feed the Confederate forces near Savannah, Georgia. However, the expedition found that the area was abandoned with only limited signs of supply movement, as the enemy had received word of the federal forces' approach and withdrew. Several buildings were destroyed, along with the ferry landing docks. A small group of African American families were brought back to Fernandina by the federal forces.

As with any large organization, the army brought people together who did not always agree. In many cases, soldiers were difficult to deal with and did not follow the articles of war or the army regulations that governed them. To deal with soldiers who were unwilling to obey the army's way of life, the Department of the South and the Military District of Florida sent them to Fernandina and Fort Clinch for hard labor punishment. Beginning in 1863, and continuing until the end of the war, hundreds of Union soldiers were sentenced by court martial to serve at the fort and towns of Old and New Fernandina. In order to maintain control of the prisoners, the provost marshal's office assigned other soldiers of the command to guard them. The prisoner labor force was so large that a company of forty soldiers supervised them as they carried out their tasks of construction work, unloading supply ships, cutting firewood and keeping up the fort and towns. In the towns, the work to extend piers for the navy, the construction of new defensive positions, repairs to the railroad and the trains was carried out by the prisoners.

Federal soldiers sentenced by court martial were used as labor forces for the towns and fort. *Courtesy of the State Archives of Florida.*

Once their time served was completed, the prisoners were either sent back to their regiments or released from the army. The following are the numbers of prisoners who were sentenced to hard labor from January to September 1864; all of them were used for labor at Fort Clinch and in the towns of Fernandina: January, 99 prisoners; February, 101 prisoners; March, 102 prisoners; April, 107 prisoners; May, 92 prisoners; June, 37 prisoners; July, 62 prisoners; August, 28 prisoners; September, 23 prisoners. Throughout 1864, there were ten deserters from the Confederate army and one Confederate prisoner of war in the custody of the federal forces.

Here at Fort Clinch, we have 101 men sentenced to hard labor. They are fed and cared for in a matter that you would think them not prisoners under punishment. They are put to work each day by the guards under the direction of Captain Sears and his engineers and are doing all matter of construction. We have them cut firewood three times a week and care for the army's mules, which are the most unpleasant animals.
—Charles Culver, Company E, First New York Engineers[20]

To manage the prisoners, the provost marshal for the Post of Fernandina issued the following order of instruction related to prisoners:

Instruction regarding prisoners sentenced to hard labor at Fort clinch, Fernandina, Florida.

1. The officer in charge of the prisoners will have the roll called at sunrise and sunset. After the calling of the roll in the morning, they will be marched to the place assigned them to wash, in single file—there will be no talking allowed—after which they will hang out their blankets, exception in rainy weather, pack and place their knapsacks at the head of their bunks and sweep out their quarters.
2. No prisoner will be allowed outside of their quarter between sunset and sunrise.
3. Sentinels will not be allowed to talk with the prisoners, except in discharge of their duty. If spoken to by them, he will immediately call the corporal of the guard.
4. The hour of labor will be regulated by the ringing of the bell.
5. No prisoners will be excused from duty, except by the doctor.
6. No talking will be allowed among the prisoners while working. No noise will be allowed in the quarters of the prisoners.

7. All prisoners will be required to bathe at least twice each week, except those excused by the doctor, and keep their beard and hair neatly trimmed.

The above instructions will be strictly adhered to, and any prisoners refusing to comply with the above instructions will be placed in solitary confinement on a bread and water diet.

By order of Nathen M. Ames, captain, Company H
7th New Hampshire Vols.
Provost Marshal[21]

Even with the large number of prisoners who were sent to Fernandina and Fort Clinch, only three were executed during the war. The three men were soldiers of the Ninety-Seventh Pennsylvania Infantry Regiment; on February 7, 1864, Privates James Wilson and James Thompson were executed by firing squad at the railroad depot in New Town Fernandina after deserting while stationed at Fernandina. They had been apprehended, tried by a military court martial and sentenced to execution by a firing squad. A third soldier of the Ninety-Seventh also deserted with Wilson and Thompson, but he was not executed until February 27, 1864. In total, four men deserted from the regiment; the fourth soldier was sentenced to a prison term of hard labor for the remainder of his enlistment.

One of the brighter times for the troops came with the arrival of any boat or ship delivering war news and mail from loved ones at home. The latest news was always two to three weeks behind, but the soldiers still enjoyed letters from family and friends who wrote about the home front. Many soldiers looked forward to receiving packages and orders they had placed from magazines and other articles.

The mail has arrived today by the Ben De Ford and consists of some three very large sacks for which I hope your letters are in, along with the package from Rebecca. Will write you tomorrow.
—Charles Culver, Company E, First New York Engineers[22]

To entertain each other, the soldiers often shared letters and gifts from home. Many also sent letters back home and placed their letters in mail sacks that were located at four different locations: Fort Clinch, army headquarters, the provost marshal's office and the harbor masters' office that was run by the navy.

Since I have arrived here, I had the opportunity to write you, Mother. The mail is collected at the fort, and when in Fernandina, I was able to send the letter off from the provost marshal's headquarters. Captain Atwater told me that letters are picked up at the pier if I should be assigned to duty there, so my letters will get sent to you.

—Henry Harrington, 157th New York[23]

Concerned for the health of the towns, post surgeon H.C. Hendricks sent a letter to the post commander with the recommendation that schools for African American children close for a period of two weeks on the account of a smallpox outbreak. A home near the lighthouse, which was visited by the soldiers, was infected, and they feared the smallpox would spread to the rest of the town and infect the command. Luckily, the sickness was minor, with only a small number of troops affected. On May 4, 1864, the following letter was sent to the provost marshal:

Headquarters Medical Dept.
Fernandina, FL, May 4, 1864
Captain J. Clayton, Atwater
Provost Marshall Fernandina

Sir: I have to report that the slaughter yard near the dock is in a very filthy state and needs policing. Also, the hides lying there about the lower dock are in a stinking condition and are very deferential to the health of the place. I would suggest that the slaughter yard be established at some point beyond the limits of the village and, if possible, so that the offence be washed off by the tides. I would further state that there is the body of a dead ox in an advanced state of decay and very offensive on the road leading to the lighthouse, near halfway to that place. There are cares of smallpox at a house near the lighthouse; it is reported that some of our soldiers not on duty there have been at the house. I further suggest that soldiers or citizens be prohibited from visiting the place, or the inmates of the house from leaving the premises until further orders.

I am very respectfully your obedient servant,
H.C. Hendricks, post surgeon[24]

On April 23, 1864, after serving for six and a half months, the 97th Pennsylvania Infantry Regiment was transferred to Port Royal, South

Carolina, and they were subsequently relieved by the 157th New York Infantry Regiment. With the arrival of the 157th, New York Infantry, Fernandina once again received a new post commander and new federal troops. The following officers were assigned to the various post positions:

Captain C.H. Vanslyke, post commander
Captain H.C. Vanderick, post surgeon
O.H. Seymore, post chaplain
H.M. Kingsberry, post quartermaster
Captain J.C. Atwater, provost marshal
Second Lieutenant W. Seton, in command of prisoners at works of Fort Clinch
First Lieutenant C.C. Burlingame, acting post adjutant
First Lieutenant R.E. Grainn, on duty with post provost marshal
Second Lieutenant C. Peirce, commanding infantry at Fort Clinch
First Lieutenant J. Ballard, commanding at the railroad bridge

The army and navy forces occupied the homes and buildings in Old and New Town, along with many runaway enslaved people who were also taking up residence in vacant homes. In Old Town Fernandina, there were three churches, nine businesses and seventy-seven homes, but only thirty-seven homes, one dry goods store and one church were in use at the time. In New Town, there were four hundred buildings; the army occupied about forty homes, and the navy used twelve homes for quartering troops. The warehouses at the docks were under navy and army control; they stored the supplies that supported the fleet and the army's quartermaster stores for the Post of Fernandina. Two of the town's churches were used as army barracks, and several homes that once belonged prominent citizens served as military headquarters. Former stores and mercantile shops were used by enterprising businessmen from the North to sell goods to the military and the civilian population. And just about every business structure was occupied by merchants or agents of the federal government.

In 1863, Miss Chloe Merrick purchased the former home of Fernandina resident and confederate general Joseph Finegan. A schoolteacher from Syracuse, New York, Miss Merrick was an abolitionist with close family ties to the Beecher Stowe family. Miss Merrick became involved in the National Freedmen Relief Association and served as a volunteer. In 1862, Miss Merrick arrived in Fernandina to establish a Freedmen's Bureau; she recognized that many Afican American children lacked shelter and education, and she

Fifteen federal infantry regiments and two engineering companies were assigned to Amelia Island over the course of the Civil War. *Courtesy of the State Archives of Florida.*

immediately set out to open and operate an orphanage and a school. The school provided education in writing, reading and arithmetic to African American children and adults. Colonel Thomas W. Osborne, the assistant commissioner of the Bureau of Refugees, Freedmen and Abandoned Lands for the state of Florida from 1865 to 1866, expressed great praise for Miss Merrick's efforts in Fernandina.

Harriet Tubman, who made two trips to Fernandina, encouraged runaway slaves to provide information on the things they had witnessed and the places they had originated from so that the federal forces could act against the Confederacy in those areas. Expeditions to the mainland helped slaves escape and provided vital information to the federal army. Tubman raised money and assisted the Freedmen's Bureau in Fernandina and the School for Colored Children, and she encouraged parents to allow their children to attend the school. She also encouraged African American males to serve in the federal army to help bring the war to an end. Her work as a nurse for people of color and federal soldiers, along with her strong voice for freedom, inspired other former slaves to enact change in the world that was needed by all people. Tubman's role was so important that the secretary of

Harriet Tubman visited Fernandina twice; there, she assisted the Freedman's Bureau and encouraged former slaves to assist the federal forces. *Courtesy of the Library of Congress.*

war, Edwin M. Stanton, gave her special permission to travel across federal lines and conduct intelligence work on behalf of the army, which helped bring the war to an end more quickly.

By July 1864, the 157th New York Infantry Regiment was relieved by the 107th Ohio, which was under the command of Major Augustus Vignos. A Battalion made up of six companies took over for the New Yorkers and secured Amelia Island. Companies A, B, F and I served at Fort Clinch, Company C was assigned to New Town Fernandina and Company E was assigned to the railroad bridge battery. The 107th also conducted mounted patrols of Amelia Island. In addition to the 107th Ohio, two companies of the 21st United States Colored Troops occupied Old Town Fernandina and the southern end of the island. In July, the 3rd and 8th USCT conducted an advance expedition and forage in Callahan, Florida, which was thirty miles west of Amelia Island and was a stop along the rail line of the Florida Railroad. After they were transported across the river by barge, the 3rd and 8th USCT moved inland, destroying supplies and bringing any person wishing for the protection of the United States to safety.

When they reached Callahan, the troops found only women, children and a few men who were unfit for military service. The rail line was not in use, and the crops in the area were too sparse to bring back to Fernandina. Unbeknownst to the Third and Eighth USCT, they were being shadowed by a Confederate home guard. With only a few shots fired, the Confederate forces were driven off, and the colored troops returned to Fernandina, along with twenty-one citizens who were seeking protection. Just one week later, on July 26, 1864, a large federal force that included the Third Rhode Island Heavy Artillery, with two field guns; the Third USCT; the Seventh USCT; the Eighth USCT; the Seventeenth Connecticut; the Thirty-Fifth USCT; and the Seventy-Fifth Ohio Mounted Infantry. The troops moved into the western part of Nassau and Duval Counties in the area known as Brandy Branch, where they were engaged by the Confederate forces that were guarding the village of Baldwin, Florida.

In August, the 34th, the 35th USCT, the 75th Ohio Mounted Infantry and the 102nd USCT conducted an attack against the Florida Railroad in the western part of the Nassau County, south of Callahan, as they believed the Confederate forces were using the railroad to move supplies and cattle toward the Florida-Georgia border and the Confederate armies further north in Georgia. Just few days later, the 102nd USCT conducted another raid on the railroad and skirmished with home guard forces. The 102nd USCT was able to destroy a portion of rail line and prevent further use by the Confederates. On August 27, 1864, most of the 107th Ohio was relieved from duty and ordered to Jacksonville, Florida. Company E and F of the regiment was to remain at Fernandina until December 1864. The 34th USCT had seen service in northeast Florida, and three companies were assigned to Fernandina and Fort Clinch. To provide additional security, the federal commander, Major Vignos of the 107th Ohio Infantry, directed the provost marshal to recruit a town militia with the following notice:

Office of the provost marshal
Fernandina, FL, October 11th, 1864

Pursuant to Special Order No. 39 from Headquarters U.S. Forces Fort Clinch Fernandina, Fla, dated Oct 5th, 1864, all able bodied men, without regard to color, residing at this post not in the army or navy of the U.S. will report at this office of the provost marshal on the 15th day of October 1864 at three o'clock p.m. for the purpose of organizing a militia company for home defense. All persons failing to report within three days after the expiration of the time allowed in this notice will be arrested and subject to punishment for violation of this order.

Samuel Miller
1st Lt, 107th Ohio Vol. Inf.
Provost Marshal[25]

In November, the military conducted a census of all the civilians in Fernandina and counted the number of males, females and children. The final counts were as follows: white males, 165; colored males, 175; white females, 76; colored females, 295; white children, 120; colored children, 423; total males, 340; total females, 371; total children, 542; and total population, 1,253. The army required all persons under the protection of the United States to take an oath of loyalty to the United States.

Over the course of the federal occupation, the following army regiments, battalions and companies served at the towns of Fernandina and at Fort Clinch:

1st New York Engineers, Companies C and E
3rd Regiment New Hampshire Infantry
4th Regiment New Hampshire Infantry
9th Regiment Maine Infantry
11th Regiment Maine Infantry

The home of former U.S. senator David L. Yulee was the headquarters for all U.S. forces on Amelia and Cumberland Islands. *Courtesy of the State Archives of Florida.*

7th Regiment Connecticut Infantry
7th Regiment New Hampshire Infantry
97th Regiment Pennsylvania Infantry
107th Regiment Ohio Infantry
157th Regiment New York Infantry
1st Regiment South Carolina Colored Infantry (designated the 33rd United States Colored Troops)
4th United States Colored Troops
8th United States Colored Troops
3rd United States Colored Troops
21st United States Colored Troops
34th United States Colored Troops
7th United States Infantry Regiment

The following officers served as commanders of Fernandina Post after it was established in 1862:

Brigadier General Horatio Wright
Colonel Richworth Rich
Colonel Joseph R. Hawley

Colonel Joseph C. Abbott
Colonel Harris M. Plaisted
Colonel Henry R. Guss
Major Galusha Pennypacker
Captain Charles Vanslyke
Major Augustine Vignos
Colonel William Arthorpe
Lieutenant Colonel William W. Marple
Captain Alfred F. Sears; chief engineer of the fort's construction; commander
*   of Company E, First New York Engineers; and commander of Fort Clinch*

The federal navy was a driving force in blockading the southern coastlines, and its operations throughout the rivers and waterways around Fernandina were great successes. The navy conducted regular patrols of the Bell River, Saint Marys River and the Cumberland River behind Cumberland Island. The navy's base of operation at the Port of Fernandina was so effective that blockade runners avoided the coast near Amelia Island. A report from August 1865, said the active navy patrols helped bring the war to a quicker end; it showed that if Fernandina had been taken by U.S. forces, the navy's ability to blockade would have been successful in the area.

With a large number of navy warships serving at Fernandina, there was a constant need for tools and supplies to refit and repair damaged vessels. These vessels allowed expeditions to confront the Confederate forces in the surrounding waterways, which was all dependent on the port of Fernandina. In addition, the navy maintained small picket boats that were regularly active in the waters around the island. The common and deep waters of the Amelia River were able to support large gatherings of ships on any given day; at any time, six to ten ships could be seen anchored, with the sailors and marines taking shore leave in Fernandina. Sailors often visited the fort, and in some cases, the warships were tied to the Fort Clinch Pier, which was just a short distance from the fort.

Admiral Samuel F. DuPont commanded the United States Navy's South Atlantic Fleet, which had temporary headquarters at Fernandina. His fleet conducted a complete blockade of the coastline from Fernandina, south, to Key West, and north, to the Virginia coast, with a major focus on operations in Charleston, South Carolina. By the summer of 1864, Admiral DuPont was replaced by Admiral John Dahlgren, who continued the navy operations of the South Atlantic Fleet. During his time in command, Admiral Dahlgren made several visits to Amelia Island, and by September 1864, the effects of

The port of Fernandina supported the federal naval blockade of the South, which helped end the war. *Courtesy of the Library of Congress.*

the navy's consistent operations along the Florida coast were successful, and portions of the blockade were lifted. The Port of Fernandina proved to be just what the navy needed, and the many improvements made by the navy benefited Fernandina as it became a major seaport in the post–Civil War timber boom.

Normal life slowly returned to the towns, as the churches that were once used as army barracks were returned to the residents, and many businesses were once again operating. The towns were booming, and life was truly starting to return to normal as the war came to an end. On May 1, 1865, news reached Fernandina that the war was over, and there was a great celebration, but it was short-lived, as word of President Lincoln's death brought sorrow. To honor the president and to celebrate the war's end, the batteries and cannons of Fort Clinch were fired in a grand salute; the flags were lowered to half-staff, and a time of mourning was held.

Although the country was in a state of mourning, it was difficult to not celebrate the surrender of Confederate forces and the capture of Richmond. The federal forces were informed to look out for anyone associated with the president's death and for Confederate leaders who were making their way south, attempting to leave the country. Since the Port of Fernandina was considered a place at which they could escape, the provost marshal increased the number of sentinels at the piers and docks. All persons arriving there were inspected and questioned on where they were traveling to and from. All ships arriving at the docks in Fernandina were subject to inspections by military forces. With the official end of the Civil War, the federal soldiers serving at Fernandina and Fort Clinch began the process of mustering out of the army and starting their lives as civilians.

3

FORT CLINCH

I n 1794, President George Washington called on Congress to provide the nation with a much-needed system of coastal defenses. During the war for America's independence, Washington and his military leaders took notice of how the invading British forces were able to make great use of the country's major waterways and seaports to land troops and supplies. To safeguard these waterways and seaports, Congress provided the funds that were needed to create the first system of forts.

Twenty-two fortifications were constructed under the direction of the army, and their placements were based on the importance of the seaports or waterways they were meant to guard. Constructed between 1794 and 1807, these new forts were no more than earthen and wood structures that contained a vast array of captured cannons of various calibers that were left over from the war for America's independence. Since these early forts were built of limited materials, constant maintenance was required.

Seeing the need to expand the fortifications to safeguard the nation's ever-increasing size, Congress authorized the construction of a second system of forts between 1808 and 1812. During this time, sixty-two forts were built from stone, brick and earth. Three types of fortifications were planned, and they were positioned again around the areas they were meant to guard. These forts often consisted of open earthen batteries; wooden, brick and earthen forts; and some brick and stone fortifications. The engineers also constructed bombproof magazines, living quarters and supplies buildings in these new fortifications. The artillery was standardized, and the same types and calibers to be used.

As the United States declared war on Great Britain in June 1812, the new forts of the second system were prepared to be tested and put to their greatest use. As they had done during the Revolution, the British attempted to capture and use the seaports and waterways to land troops and supplies. In Baltimore, Maryland, the British came up against Fort McHenry, which held the British fleet at bay under the command of Vice Admiral Alexander Cochrane. It was during this battle that Francis Scott Key wrote the poem "The Defense of Fort McHenry," which later became the lyrics to the "Star-Spangled Banner," the country's national anthem. Fort McHenry held out, and the British fleet left after it was unable to enter the harbor or force the fort to surrender.

In 1794, President Washington pressed Congress for funds to construct forts to guard America's waterways and seaports. *Courtesy of the Library of Congress.*

The British did make several successful landings and were able to capture Washington, D.C., which forced President Madison and his wife to evacuate, with Dolly Madison carrying the portrait of George Washington to safety. The British proceeded to burn the White House and portions of the capital city. With the end of the war in 1812, the United States saw yet another need to improve the country's defenses.

Under President Madison's administration, Congress funded a third system of forts. To oversee this project, a fortification board was created with the following officers: Brigadier General Joseph Swift, Colonel William McRee, Lieutenant Colonel Joseph G. Totten, Captain J.D. Elliott of the U.S. Navy, former French general Simon Bernard, and, later, civil engineer John Sullivan, whose expertise lied in the nations waterways. The board took notice of the major seaports that needed to be guarded and the other ports and waterways that were rapidly becoming important. Ultimately, forty-two locations were selected to receive forts, and they were constructed using the most permanent materials: stone, brick and cast iron. Many of the forts were tiered structures with multiple levels of artillery rising to heights of fifty-five feet and walls that were eight to twelve feet thick. Bombproof powder magazines were built to secure the thousands of pounds of cannon powder that were needed to fire the large number of cannons that were mounted in the forts. The project was a major undertaking by the corps of engineers,

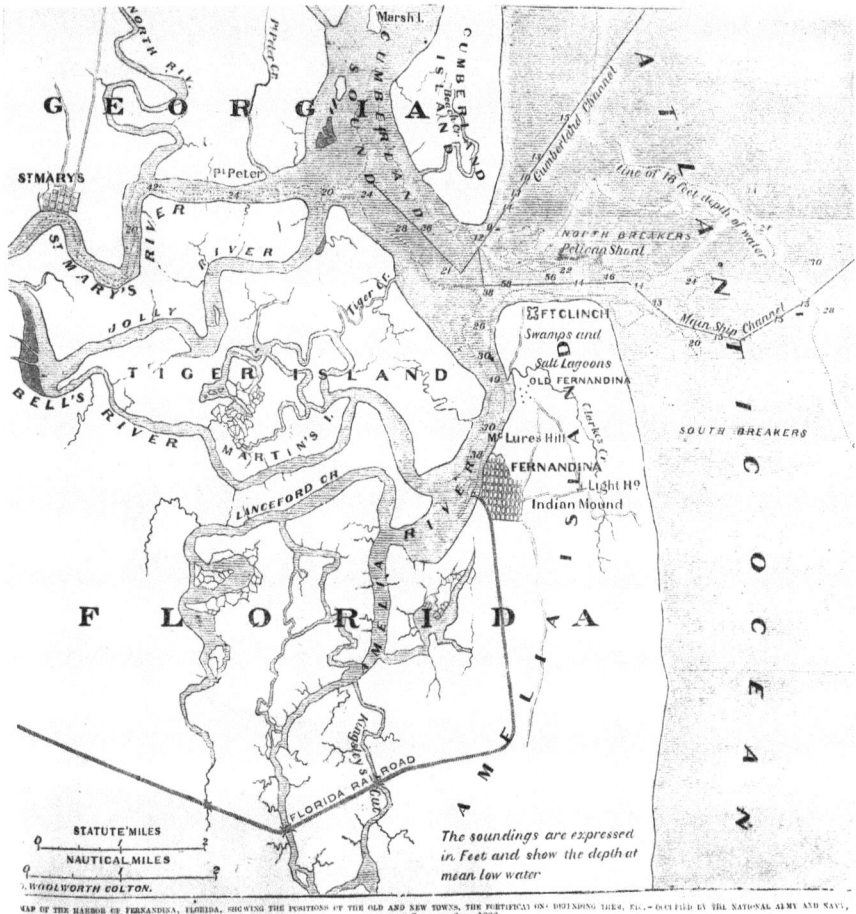

From 1816 to 1867, forty-two third system fortifications were built; nine were constructed in Florida. *Courtesy of the State Archives of Florida.*

and it was given the utmost attention, as the survival of the nation during an invasion depended on it.

In Florida, the corps recommended that seven locations receive the new forts and that two additional defense towers be constructed later. Under the Adam-Onis Treaty of 1819, Spain seceded Florida to the United States in 1821. With Florida now a U.S. territory, the U.S. Army Corps of Engineers began a survey of the Florida coast, examining the major waterways, seaports and coastal towns and cities. By 1820, the fortification board was reduced by two with the resignation of General Swift and Colonel McRee. Captain Elliott of the U.S. Navy, Lieutenant Colonel Totten and General Bernard of the U.S. Army were left to carry on with the designs and placements of the new forts. Swift and McRee resigned after the appointment of Simon Bernard to the board; in 1816, Bernard was offered a general's commission in the U.S. Army by President Madison with the understanding that Bernard would direct the efforts of the fortification board. Swift and McRee could not tolerate Bernard leading the board, as they felt that they were the senior officers and understood the best course to follow in the defense of the country. General Simon Bernard was a career officer who graduated from Ecole Polytechnique, had already designed several forts in Europe and had served as an aide-de-camp to Napoleon. With the defeat of Napoleon, Bernard was forced to leave France. And with America looking to build a new system of forts, President Madison was encouraged by James Barbour, the senate committee chairman for military affairs, to accept Bernard and give him a key position on the board of fortification.

After a complete study of the Florida coast, selections were made, and plans were drafted for the third-system forts in Florida. The construction of the forts in Pensacola was started before Florida became a state; this was followed by the construction of the forts in the Florida Keys, which occurred just after Florida became a state in March 1845. Under President John Tyler, in 1842, the federal government purchased property at the north end of Amelia Island. The tracts of land were obtained from the Clark and McQueen families, and an additional property was purchased from George Fairbanks. This meant the federal government owned the entirety of the north end of Amelia Island; 1,100 acres were needed to build the fort and secure and protect the Cumberland Sound and the connecting waterways.

In 1831, General Simon Bernard resigned his position, leaving Colonel Joseph G. Totten to carry on directing, planning and building the third-system forts. Totten graduated from West Point in 1805 and was commissioned into the corps of engineers, where he was assigned to construct America's second-system forts. During the War of 1812, Totten saw extensive military service, and by the end of the war, he had been promoted to lieutenant colonel for gallantry in combat. After he was appointed to the fortification board in 1816, Bernard designed and directed several third-system forts to be constructed. With the departure of Bernard, Totten continued the board's work, and in 1838, he was appointed chief of the U.S. Army's Corps of Engineers, a position he would hold until his death on April 22, 1864. During the Mexican War, Totten was promoted to brigadier general for his gallantry and meritorious service during the Siege of Vera Cruz. In addition to his military service, Totten was the cofounder of the National

Major General Joseph G. Totten served as chief of the army corps of engineers and designed Fort Clinch. *Courtesy of the Library of Congress.*

Academy of Science and a regent of the Smithsonian. For his service to the nation, President Abraham Lincoln promoted Totten to major general just before his passing, and upon his death, the president called for thirty days of mourning for the honored soldier and American.

Under General Totten, the design plans were created for Fort Clinch. Beginning in 1844 and through 1858, engineer officers who were working in the office of the corps of engineers drafted the construction plans. Additional plans for Fort Clinch were created in 1864 under the direction of General Richard Delifield, the new chief of the corps of engineers, and further designs were created between 1865 and 1878 to modernize the fort. Starting in 1847, a civilian work force was hired, and notices were placed in local towns to say that the government was hiring experienced tradesmen. In addition to the hired civilian work forces, slave labor was used. The United States Army did not hire slaves; instead, it offered contracts to civilians to provide the needed work, which allowed slave owners the opportunity to obtain the contracts and use their slaves to conduct the work.

On November 22, 1847, two construction projects commenced, and at the same time, the pier and ground-clearing work at the fort site began. A labor force of both paid workers and slaves began building what would be Fort Clinch, and by May 1848, the pier was ready to receive construction materials. The ground was leveled and prepared for the foundations to be bored between the fall of 1849 and early 1850. After the pier was completed, a road to connect the fort site with Old Town Fernandina was built. The road was just one and a quarter mile long and provided workers and supply carriers with easier access to the fort. A small community sprouted up next to the construction site, as workers and their families lived on site.

Major George Dutton served as the first engineer officer of Fort Clinch after he was commissioned into the corps of engineers in 1822 upon his graduation from West Point. Lieutenant Dutton worked on several third-system forts and was respected by Totten and other senior officers. When the construction of Fort Clinch began, Dutton was serving as a regional engineer officer with the rank of captain, and he was overseeing several army engineering projects in Florida. As the chief engineer, Dutton was assigned, along with an assistant engineer officer, to live in Fernandina and directly supervise the construction of the fort. A civilian foreman directed the work parties and maintained control over the tools, machinery and animals used in the construction; hired in 1858, J.A. Walker was Fort Clinch's civilian foreman and keeper.

To construct the fort, a combination of martials were selected. Due to the lack of clay for brickmaking in Florida, engineers sought contracts with brick providers in nearby Georgia. Also absent from Florida was hard stone; to overcome this, additional contracts were set up with various rock quarries in the north. The bricks used to build Fort Clinch came from two brickyards: the Hermitage Yard at Savannah, Georgia, which was used from 1847 to 1861, and the brickyard located on the Saint Marys River known as Brick Yard Landing. The brick yard was owned by Samuel Swann, a local resident of Fernandina, who, in 1856, acquired the brick yard and sold bricks known as savannah grays from 1856 to 1861. With the outbreak of the Civil War, all work on Fort Clinch halted, and during the Confederate occupation, no construction was carried out on the fort by southern forces. However, the southern troops did clear a portion of the parade field to allow for a camp to be set up, and they made use of the guardroom, prison and carpenter shop. With the capture and occupation of Amelia Island by the federal forces, construction resumed, with a focus on completing the fort. Unable to acquire Georgia bricks from Savannah and Brick Yard Landing, the federal army opened contracts with northern brickyards. The north river brick yards located on the Hudson River, just north of New York City, and the Philadelphia Brickyard provided bricks to Fort Clinch from 1862 to 1867. These bricks were light and dark red in color and were smaller than the bricks that were brought in from Georgia before the Civil War.

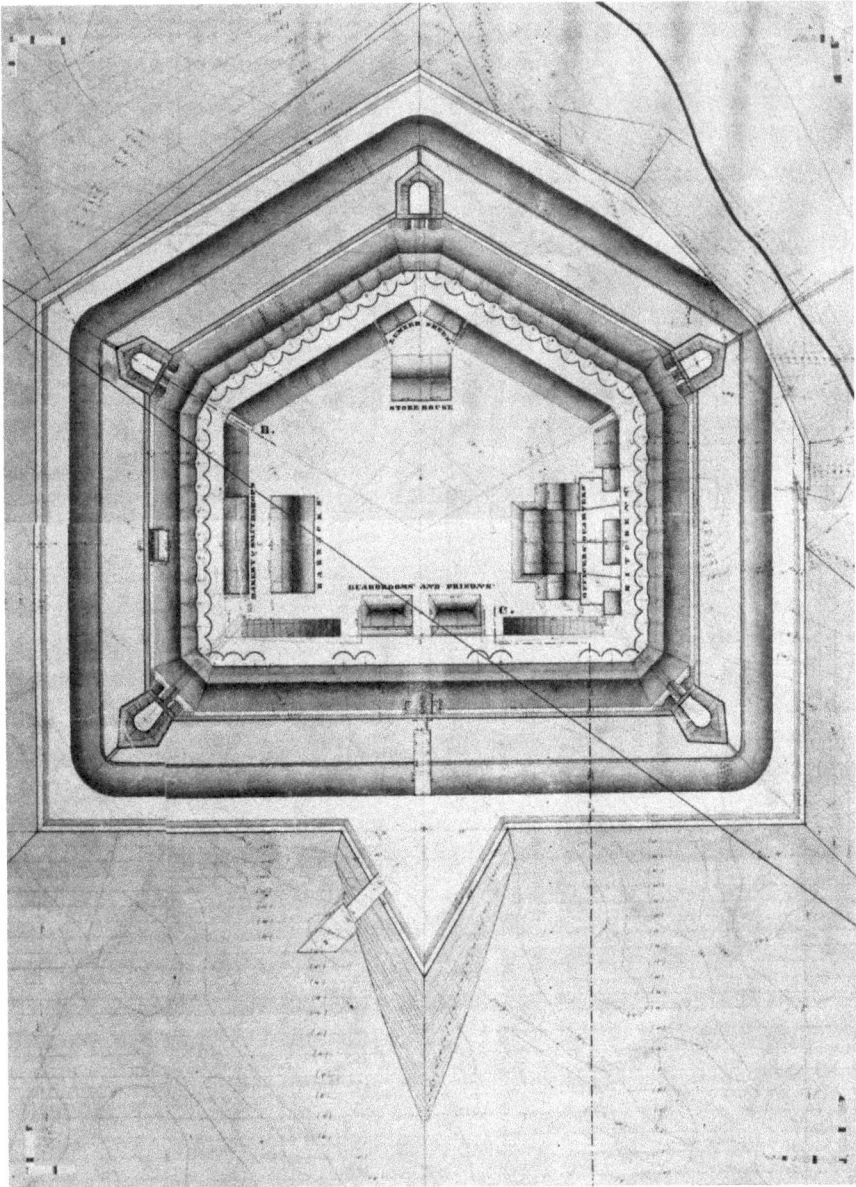

Fort Clinch served in three wars and was intended to accommodate five hundred troops and seventy-seven cannons. *Courtesy of the Library of Congress.*

Granite was acquired from Durham, New Hampshire, for windowsills, lentils on the buildings, staircases, cannon platforms, and the fort's main entranceway, which was located at the drawbridge. Slate stone acquired from Pennsylvania and New York was used as flooring in the nine galleries and bastions, and a large amount was used on the cannon mounts in addition to granite. Pennsylvania brown sandstone was used to mount the hinges and locks for the bastion doors, shutters and gallery doors. The roofs of the barracks, guardroom, prison and storehouse buildings were made of slate stone shingles, and the kitchen, bakery, farrier, blacksmith and carpenter shops had tin roofs coated in pitch.

Cast iron, a new type of building material, was incorporated into the fort's construction and was used in the soldiers' barracks and storehouse building to support the arched brick ceilings on the first levels of both buildings; it was also used to make roof trestles in both structures. Box beams, which were made of cast iron and bolted together, supported the roof of the veranda of the soldiers' barracks. Located in the eaves of the barracks building were two large iron-plated tanks that were used to collect rainwater for drinking; this also meant that there was running water in the barracks. All five bastions and cannon embrasures were also made of cast iron. Some of the most impressive cast-iron pieces in the fort were the eighteen Corinthian columns that were used to support the overhang roofs of the guardroom and prison buildings, along with the veranda of the soldiers' barracks.

Since wood was needed for the fort's construction, the engineers contracted with a local sawmill that was located about a mile away from the fort in Old Fernandina. Reid's Mill was the main supplier of timber for Fort Clinch from 1848 to 1860. After the abandonment of Fernandina by its residents, Reid's Sawmill was not in operation. To overcome this, engineers installed a new steam engine and began operating the sawmill once again. Although most building materials were shipped in, tabby concrete was made locally and used in the fort's foundations, walls, bastions and cannon platform bases. With a large crop of oyster shells on Amelia Island, the engineers made great use of them in the production of tabby; they burned the shells in kilns, mixed in water, broke the shells down into a lime paste, added oyster shells as an aggregate, along with a little sand, and made a pliable concrete. To ensure a strong foundation, the engineers used tabby to make three- to four-foot-thick foundations for the building's walls and bastions.

Fort Clinch was designed in the shape of a truncated hexagon or an irregular pentagon; it was five sided, with curtain walls that were twenty-six feet high, five feet thick at the base and four and a half feet thick at the top.

Fort Clinch's main artillery was planned to hold fifty-seven seacoast heavy cannons and twenty twenty-four-pound flank casemate howitzers. *Courtesy of the State Archives of Florida.*

Five bastions were placed at the connections of two walls; they were eight feet thick and thirty-six feet tall. The fort's interior contained two separate barracks: one for enlisted men and one for officers. It also had four kitchens, a quartermaster supply building, guardrooms, a prison, a bakery, carpenter shops and blacksmith and farrier shops. There were five main powder magazines that were used to store forty thousand pounds of cannon powder, and there were four magazines that were used to store ready munitions of powder bags and exploding shells for the artillery. Twenty-two latrines allowed human waste to be removed from the fort by a series of drainages systems. Eleven cisterns stored fifty-three thousand gallons of drinking water. The fort was slated to accommodate a garrison of five hundred artillery soldiers to operate and man the seventy-seven cannons, fifty-seven heavy offense cannons and twenty defense cannons.

The fort's construction was expected to cost $1 million, take fifteen to twenty years to complete and use a total of seven million bricks. In addition to the fort itself, the outer works of Fort Clinch consisted of a glacis that served as a counterscarp to the main curtain walls. This glacis, an earthen embankment, rose to a height of twenty-two to twenty-four feet and encompassed the fort. The glacis masked the fort's walls from direct view and provided protection from enemy artillery fire. A seawall that was twelve feet high and five feet thick was constructed outside the fort's main walls and stretched from the east bastion to the northwest bastion, protecting the fort's outer walls and glacis from stormy seas and the Cumberland Sound.

Located just behind the glacis and seawalls, and directly in front of the fort's main curtain walls, was a dry ditch that provided a low point in front of the fort's five outer brick walls and allowed for artillery and rifle fire to sweep the ditch, wounding or killing anyone who was in the ditch or attempting to climb the walls. The dry ditch, which was never intended to be a moat, did allow for drainage of excess water from inside the fort. To enter and leave the fort, the engineers constructed a sally port in the south face curtain wall, which was also known as the gorge wall, as it was the longest of the five walls, with a length of about 500 feet (all the other walls were about 240 feet long).

Unlike many of the third-system forts built during this period, Fort Clinch was designed by General Totten to mount its main batteries of artillery on top of its ramparts, which measured forty feet wide at the base and rose twenty feet. An en barbette was constructed to mount cannons, and a parapet wall was built in front of it to protect the artillery and cannoneers from enemy fire. A terreplein that was located at the back of the artillery allowed for the troops to safely move along the top of the fort. To access the top of the fort and to move artillery, ammunitions and troops, two large service ramps were constructed as part of the original design; one was located on the east side, next to the guardroom, and the other was located on the south side, next to the prison. In addition to the service ramps, nine granite stone staircases were built to allow troops to move from the parade field to the terreplein and cannon positions.

Located along the length of the curtain walls and within the five bastions, 126 firing ports, also referred to as loopholes, were built for musket fire. These loopholes allowed the fort's defenders to rain down rifle fire on assaulting enemies. The walkway behind the curtain walls was called a *chemin de' ronde*, meaning a place to walk. The curtain wall was referred to by the engineers of Fort Clinch as a Carnot wall, in reference of the French designer. Much of Fort Clinch's design was based on French designs, as were the designs of so many of the forts that were being built during the nineteenth century. Because of this, many of the words used to describe the forts are French.

To honor Brigadier General Duncan L. Clinch, the United States War Department, in General Order No. 38, dated November 4, 1850, named the fort that was under construction Fort Clinch. General Clinch was born in Nash County, North Carolina, in 1787 to Mary and Colonel Joseph J. Clinch. The general was raised in Tarboro, North Carolina, and his parents passed away while he was still young. His father's brother and wife raised him and his brother. Clinch received his education at the Tarboro Male Academy where he excelled in reading, writing and mathematics and regularly attended church fostering his strong religious convictions.

Fort Clinch was named for Brigadier General Duncan Lamont Clinch on November 4, 1850, by General Order 38 of the war department. *Courtesy of the Library of Congress.*

At the age of twenty, Clinch was looking for a career in the Untied State Army, and after about a year, his opportunity came when a congressman from his state was required to recommend two men to be appointed officers in the army. Clinch accepted the opportunity and was commissioned a first lieutenant; he was assigned to the Third United States Infantry and served in New Orleans, Louisiana. While he was serving as a company officer, he held other duties within the regiment and military post; he served as a company paymaster, a quartermaster for the post and an adjutant and company drill officer for recruits. By 1810, he was promoted to captain and company commander and was assigned to Baton Rouge. With the outbreak of the War of 1812, Captain Clinch, along with his company, was transferred to New York, and after serving there for a year, Clinch was promoted to lieutenant colonel at Plattsburg, New York, on August 4, 1813.

After he was placed in command of Camp Lake Erie, he oversaw the day-to-day operations of the camp along with the training and preparation of the troops. While serving there, he participated in limited engagements against the British. With the end of the War of 1812, Clinch was transferred to South Georgia. As tensions rose along the Florida–Georgia border, Clinch oversaw military operations against the African American fort, which was known as the Negro Fort. During an engagement with the African American fort, the naval gunfire destroyed it, and the occupants were either killed or taken prisoner. Following his duty there, Clinch was transferred to Saint Marys, Georgia, where he served as post commander at Point Peter. On April 20, 1819, Clinch was promoted to colonel, and on June 1, 1821, Clinch assumed command of the Fourth Infantry Regiment. For ten years of faithful service in one grade, Colonel Clinch advanced to the rank of brevet brigadier general on April 20, 1829, and took command of military operations in Florida.

When the United States government looked to remove the Seminole people from the Territory of Florida, General Clinch assumed military command and operations. Once he was promoted to the rank of full brigadier general, Clinch directed the military in the removal of the Seminoles. With uprisings from the Seminoles, General Clinch led a military force of regulars and Florida militia in the Battle of the Withlacoochee, which was ultimately a victory over the natives. Unable to agree with the government over the handling of the native and after serving twenty-eight years in the army, Clinch resigned from the U.S. Army in September 1836.

In his personal life, Brigadier General Clinch was married three times. He married his first wife, Eliza B. McIntosh, in 1819, and the couple had eight children. With the death of his first wife in 1835, Clinch married Elizabeth B. Houston in 1836. Elizabeth passed away in 1838, and for the next ten years, Clinch remained a widower. In 1846, he married Sophia Hermes Gibbs Couper, and their marriage lasted until his death. During his years of civilian life, Clinch operated a rice plantation known as Refuge; it was located in Georgia on the Satilla River. He also maintained a second home in Clarksville, Georgia, that was known as the Summer House. In addition to the Refuge Plantation, Clinch owned Auld Lang Syne Plantation near Micanopy, Florida, which grew sugarcane and produced rum.

Clinch was later asked to serve on the examining board for the United States Military Academy. In this position, General Clinch interviewed and counseled young men who were looking to be admitted to the West Point Military Academy. He later became involved in the politics of the time and served in the U.S. Congress in 1844. He also sought to become governor of Georgia and ran for office; however, he was unsuccessful in winning the governorship. He then returned to private life, and on November 27, 1849, Brigadier General Duncan L. Clinch passed away in Macon, Georgia. He was laid to rest at Bonaventure Cemetery after a grand funeral, where thousands turned out to pay their respects; full military honors were rendered, with senior army leaders and the governor of Georgia giving moving invocations.

By 1860, two of the five Carnot walls (curtain walls) had been completed, along with the north bastion. The remaining walls were half done, and the other four bastions were in various stages of construction. In the fort, the guardroom, prison, carpenter shops, latrines and one service ramp had been completed. The quartermaster storehouse was finished just above the first-story windows, and the doors of the kitchen pantries and four service magazines were just finishing up. Foundations were being laid for the bakery and the farrier and blacksmith shops. The seawalls were built, and the sally port (main entrance) side walls were just completed. Outside, the dry ditch was just being finished, and the glacis was rising to its full height. The fort was beginning to take shape.

To support the garrison of soldiers, the engineers planned for the fort to operate with little to no assistance from the outside for a period of sixty to ninety days, thereby making it self-sufficient. A quartermaster sergeant was assigned to the storehouse operations, as it was one of the three most important structures within the fort, along with the powder magazines

Fort Clinch could store forty thousand to fifty thousand pounds of cannon powder and fifty-three thousand gallons of fresh drinking water. *Courtesy of the State Archives of Florida.*

and cisterns that held fresh drinking water. The quartermaster building, or storehouse as it was sometimes referred to, was located on the parade field's northwest side. It was a two-story structure divided into eleven rooms; each room was designed to store and hold different types of supplies. Five rooms were located on the first level and consisted of an office, a room for clothing and accoutrements for soldiers and rooms with barrels of oils, paint, liquid supplies, tools, engineering equipment, small arms, ammunition and stored field rations. The second story housed clothing and the soldiers' equipment, additional tools, engineering items, cookware, tin ware, additional barrels of lamp oil, paint and lacquers. The structure's construction began in 1858, with the laying of its foundation, and work continued until the summer of 1860. The building was brought to a level of construction just above the first-floor windows and doors. The second story was completed in 1863. The storehouse was not fully finished until 1866, but it was completed enough to be used from 1863 to 1865.

The fort's dispensary was established in December 1863 in the second story of the northwest corner, and it was staffed by hospital stewards until September 1864. The following stewards were assigned to the dispensary to provide medical care: John Y.M. Carter, Jacob W. Mangold, John Page, Rufus Godfrey and William Langford. If care was required above their training, the sick or injured were transferred to the post hospital in town, and in some cases, the town's army physician would travel to the fort. From December 1863 to September 1864, hospital stewards saw to the daily medical care of the soldiers at the fort.

To accomodate the troops, two large barracks were built, and the officers' and associated administrators' rooms were located in the officers' quarters. The main enlisted barracks were constructed between 1863 and 1867 and were divided into four main quarters; the sergeants had a separate living space with private and semiprivate rooms, and the corporals and musicians were quartered together, with separate rooms housing some thirty privates on the first story. On the second story, two large open rooms were able to accommodate forty-eight to fifty-six men each. When the barracks were fully occupied, they could quarter between 125 and 150 soldiers. The back of the barracks had a porch on the first story and a veranda on the second story, and the second level of the barracks could be accessed by an internal staircase in the center of the building. To keep the barracks comfortable, large doors and windows allowed air to pass through, and the high ceiling allowed hot air to rise, keeping the lower portions cool. An advanced water system was installed and allowed for running water in the barracks. The

The barracks of Fort Clinch were constructed between 1863 and 1867 could accommodate 150 soldiers. *Courtesy of the State Archives of Florida.*

water was provided by two large iron tanks that were placed in the attic space; they stored rainwater that could be accessed by a series of pipes and faucets. The construction of the barracks began after Fort Clinch was occupied by First New York Engineers, and the barracks were built using New York and Pennsylvania red bricks and New Hampshire granite.

I have a small, quaint room on the first story of the barracks, where I spend a great amount of time handling the company papers. It's a pleasant room, and I am greeted by the sunrise and have the honor to gaze upon the flag of our country.

Hebal, you ask of my living condition here. It is a comfortable one. We have moved from the quarters outside the fort to inside; however, the sand is quite a problem. When the breeze from the sea comes in the afternoon, it moves it all about. For myself, I have a room with a nice window and no one to share with, as I did outside the fort.

—Sergeant George D. Hughes, Company E, First New York Engineers[26]

With four kitchens and a bakery, the soldiers of Fort Clinch were provided with daily meals, and each of the four kitchens contained a pantry for food storage. The pantries were able to accommodate fresh and dried vegetables, dry goods and meats. The kitchens were under construction from 1858 to 1860, but the work was halted until 1862, which brought the kitchens to a level of completion. To prepare the meals, each kitchen had a small beehive oven along with a fireplace and a pot crane to hang kettles and cook buckets over the fire. Each kitchen could serve a company of one hundred soldiers. Fresh meat was available to the troops, as the slaughter yards for cattle and hogs were located in New Town at the docks. The slaughter yard was moved south of the town in 1864. Each afternoon, the slaughtering commenced, and by the next morning, the fresh meat was delivered to the federal troops on Amelia Island. Arriving at the fort in the early morning, before sunrise, the wagon from the slaughter yard delivered fresh meat to the fort for the day's rations; large curing barrels in the pantries and kitchens preserved the meat until it was cooked. To oversee the cooking, the soldiers voted two to three men from there company to serve as their cooks. The bakery behind the enlisted barracks was constructed between 1862 and 1864 and provided the fort's garrison with flour goods. Two large ovens were heated to the required temperature for baking bread, biscuits and gingerbread, along with some treats of pies, cookies and sweetbread. Six soldiers were assigned to the bakery, and they worked day and night for three to four days a week, baking goods for a seven-day week.

To maintain the fort and make repairs as they were needed, the engineers constructed three workshops in the fort; they were located behind the quartermaster building. The carpenter shops and lumber sheds were constructed between 1856 and 1860 and allowed for all types of woodworking. The blacksmith and farrier shops were built between 1862 and 1864 and were vital to the fort. The blacksmith shop was used to make and repair ironwork, and the farrier shop provided upkeep for the mules and horses, including shoeing and saddle and tack repairs. Located just outside the fort's west wall, the stables kept up to twenty-four mules and horses, along with storage of tack, saddles, feed and hay, along with wagons and carts that were needed for fort use.

Beginning in the fall of 1863, the engineers began pouring foundations for the officer's barracks, and by 1864, the walls had risen just above the first-floor windows and doors of the officer's quarters when construction was halted in the summer of 1864. The officers' barracks were never completed, and the walls that were in place were removed to be used in the construction of a new gun platform and protective wall in 1898.

Fort Clinch had a state-of-the-art latrine system, with a total of twenty-two latrines constructed and located on three sides of the fort. On the east side, next to the service powder magazines, eight officers' latrines were constructed between 1862 and 1864. These latrines were connected to the ocean and were flooded with seawater during tide change to remove waste. Additionally, the officers' latrines were flushed out each time it rained;

Fort Clinch, which was intended to guard and defend the Cumberland Sound and the seaports of Saint Mary's Georgia and Fernandina, Florida. *Courtesy of the State Archives of Florida.*

rainwater landed on the roofs of the kitchens and was channeled to run into the latrines. Located behind the quartermasters' storehouse, four enlisted latrines were built between 1856 and 1860 and functioned with the same tide and rainwater flushing. Ten additional enlisted latrines with tin trough urinals were constructed on the southwest curtain wall between 1862 and 1864. The roof over the latrine room directed rainwater to flush both the trough and the latrine room, where soldiers would sit on a bench to relieve themselves. The waste was washed into a drainage system that was placed outside the curtain wall and underground.

The five bastions of Fort Clinch were built to defend the fort's outer walls, and they served as main powder magazines, allowing for forty thousand pounds of cannon powder to be kept in them. Their walls were made with tabby concrete and faced with bricks; they were five to eight feet thick and thirty-six feet high. The cisterns built under the flooring collect rainwater, which contributed to the total freshwater storage of the fort. The main room of the bastions held four model 1844 twenty-four-pound flank howitzers;

two of them were located on each flank of the bastion and allowed for firing along the fort's outer walls and through the dry ditch, thereby creating a deadly crossfire. Each bastion was topped with a smooth-bore Columbiad cannon or rifle cannon that was installed on the cannon platform center-pintle artillery mount, which allowed for a 360-degree traverse. Model 1844 eight-inch Columbiads were installed on top of three of the fort's bastions by the end of 1863; the east, north and northwest bastions served as offensesive and defensive weapons. To access the top of the bastions, a spiral staircase was built from the lower level to the top of the bastion. The fort had the unique ability to secure the bastions with heavy wooden doors and shutters covered in iron plates; this sealed the bastion from any person attempting to enter. From the top of each of the five bastions, soldiers had a clear field for small-arms fire along the outer and interior walls and outward from the bastion tops. Each bastion was fort unto itself.

Fort Clinch was meant to have seventy-seven cannons; fifty-two seacoast cannons of smooth bore or rifle bore were meant to be installed at the top of the five rampart walls on en barbettes (cannon platforms), another five seacoast cannons were to be mounted on top of each bastion and twenty flank howitzers were divided among the five bastions, with four howitzers mounted to each. Field artillery was issued as needed to the fort, with two to four field guns creating a two-gun section or four-gun battery. The field artillery could be moved around the fort or taken outside, if required. In a report from Colonel H.S. Putman in May 1863, the following cannons were listed as being located and mounted at Fort Clinch:

Three eight-inch Columbiads
Eight thirty-two-pounders
Six twenty-four-pounders
Eight twenty-four-pound flank howitzers
One six-inch (Rebel) rifle cannon
Total: twenty-six cannons

The following list came directly from Captain Alfred F. Sears, Fort Clinch's commanding officer. He listed the types and number of cannons mounted in the fort as of August 24, 1863.

Ten thirty-two-pounders
Three eight-inch Columbiads
Six twenty-four-pounders

By September 1865, Fort Clinch had thirty-four pieces of mounted artillery. *Courtesy of the Library of Congress.*

Eight twenty-four-pound flank howitzers
One six-inch (Rebel) rifle cannon
Total: twenty-eight cannons

Another list of artillery from December 31, 1863, written by Captain F.M. Guss shows Fort Clinch had:

Seven twenty-four-pound siege guns
Ten thirty-two-pound siege guns
Three eight-inch Columbiads
Eight twenty-four-pound howitzers in flank defense

In all of the aforementioned artillery reports, one piece of artillery is listed as a six-inch (Rebel) rifle. This captured rifle cannon was mounted in the fort but was always noted in reports as a captured Rebel rifle cannon. Its caliber was that of a converted forty-two-pounder made from smooth bore to rifle bore, and it was reclassified as an eighty-four-pounder. The total number of artilleries reported was twenty-nine cannons. In June 1864, the reports added one ten-pound Parrott rifle on field carriage and one twenty-four-pound field howitzer that was also mounted on field carriage; this brought the total to thirty-one cannons located at Fort Clinch. By September 1865, the following artillery were in place. To provide for a lack of rifle artillery, Charles T. James invented a system that allowed for smooth-bore cannons to be converted into rifled cannons; it was known as the James System of Rifling. A number of these cannons were installed at Fort Clinch during the federal occupation.

Three eight-inch Columbiads
Seven thirty-two-pounders, smooth bore
One twenty-four-pond field howitzer on field carriage
Seven twenty-four-pound smooth-bore siege guns
Eight twenty-four-pound flank howitzers
Four thirty-two-pounders, rifled
One ten-pound Parrott gun (rifle) on field carriage
Two twenty-four-pound siege guns, rifled
One six-inch (Rebel) rifle (eighty-four pounder)
Total: 34 cannons.

On March 3, 1862, the First New York Engineers arrived at Fort Clinch; Company C was assigned to the fort and resumed construction. In February 1863, Company C was transferred to Beufort, South Carolina, and Company E assumed the forts construction. Captain Alfred F. Sears was then appointed the chief engineer of the fort's construction by orders of the War Department and the corps of engineers, dated March 1862. The First Regiment New York Engineers was the brainchild of Colonel Edward W. Serrell, a prominent civil engineer from New York. Colonel Serrell saw the need to organize and recruit a regiment of skilled artisans for service to the Union; he mostly wanted men from the state of New York, but four companies were recruited in New Jersey. With its organization complete, the regiment consisted of twelve companies, making it one of the largest regiments of engineers in the U.S. Army. The regiment was sent to Washington, D.C., where it saw brief service before heading to Hampton Road, Virginia's Fortress Monroe; it then went to Hilton Head, South Carolina, where it became the engineer force for the Department of the South. Many of the regiment's companies were assigned to different locations along the South Carolina, Georgia and Florida coasts. Companies C and E were assigned to Fernandina and Fort Clinch. With orders to rejoin the regiment and move to Virginia in the spring of 1864, Captain Sears retained a small detachment of soldiers from Company E to assist in the continued construction of Fort Clinch until the end of the war.

The engineer companies were comprised of 4 officers, 1 captain, 2 first lieutenants and 1 second lieutenant. The noncommissioned officers consisted of 10 sergeants, 10 corporals, 60 privates first class and 60 privates, for a total of 144 officers and men. The privates were divided between master craftsmen and those with limited trade skills. The skilled men and artisans consisted of bricklayers; stone cutters; blacksmiths; tinsmiths; coppersmiths; wheelwrights; staircase makers; mechanics; carpenters, both finished and rough; farriers; carriage makers; coopers; and window and door makers, along with others who had necessary skills for the time.

Captain Alfred F. Sears served at Fort Clinch from March 1862 to January 1866 as the commanding officer of Company E of the First New York Engineers, the chief engineer of Fort Clinch's construction and as the fort's

From March 1862 to 1865, soldiers of the First New York Engineers carried out the construction of Fort Clinch. *Courtesy of the Library of Congress.*

commander. Born in Boston, Massachusetts, on November 26, 1826, Sears attended public school, where he won a Franklin Medal scholarship. Upon his graduation from the Winthrop School in 1841, he went on to attend the English High School, where he graduated in 1844. In 1845, he entered a mercantile counting house, and in 1846, he went on to the architect's offices for further schooling. There, he studied a special course of mathematics that was taught by the famed Master Sherwin.

Following his schooling, Sears went on to work for the Boston Waterworks, where he worked under the distinguished civil engineer E.S. Chesbrough. Captain Sears was later connected to the Cheshire Railroad of New Hampshire and became resident engineer of the Baltimore and Ohio Railroad under the late B.H. Latrobe. With the outbreak of the Civil War, Alfred F. Sears went to work as a surveyor in Newark, New Jersey. In June 1861, he resigned from his surveying job to raise a company of skilled craftsmen for the First Regiment of Engineers, which was accepted for service and became Company E of the First New York Engineers. He was commissioned as captain of the company, and in October, he joined the expeditionary forces under command of Brigadier General Thomas W. Sherman. He was part of the federal forces to capture Hilton Head, and Forts Walker and Beauregard at Port Royal, South Carolina. Following the federal operation there, he was assigned to Brigadier General Horatio G. Wright's expedition to capture and occupy Fernandina and Fort Clinch, where he was elevated to the position of engineer in charge of the renewed construction. While he was at the fort, he moved forward with the continued work in the hopes of completing the fort in approximately two years.

Later, in 1862, Captain Sears went to Washington, D.C., where he met with General Joseph Totten, the chief of the corps of engineers. After a week of consultation with General Totten, he was granted leave to New York to open additional contracts for construction materials and to visit with family and friends. During his visit, he received dispensation of the grand lodge of New York to become a master mason in the Kane Lodge of New York. Following his visit, he finished his contracts on behalf of the army for Fort Clinch and returned to Fernandina. While he was in the service of the federal army and given the responsibility to oversee the war-time construction of Fort Clinch, he was one of only a few volunteer officers to be permitted to report directly to General Totten.

In January 1865, Captain Sears was promoted to the rank of major. With the end of the war in May 1865, and with his regiment mustering out of service, Major Sears was asked by the new commander of the corps of engineers,

General Richard Delifield, to remain in service for an additional six months and possibly until January 1866—he agreed. Under his direction, 2.5 million bricks were put in place, along with a large portion of artillery mounted in the fort. His direction of the construction work brought Fort Clinch to a level of near completion. Following his discharge, Major Sears went on to oversee the building of the Belleville Reservoir as assistant engineer of Newark, New Jersey Water Works. Following this project, he was elected chief engineer of the Newark and New York Railroad. Years later, he oversaw the engineering operations of the New York Railroad's expansion and went on to construct railroads in Mexico, Peru and Costa Rica. A talented army engineer officer and civil engineer, Major Sears was a driving force in the construction of Fort Clinch from 1862 to 1866.

With a company of engineer soldiers carrying out the work needed to move toward the completion of the fort, Captain Sears saw the opportunity to employ a civilian work force of both skilled and unskilled laborers, along with a large group of former slaves, both skilled and unskilled, who needed a source of income to support their families. Captain Sears employed many former slaves and set out to use them in the continued work on the fort, and he paid them accordingly with wages and rations. From August 1862 to the brief halt of work in 1864, and from the resumption of construction later that year until the end of the war, the fort's construction was coming to a rapid end. More than eighty civilians were employed, and more were hired in 1864; this brought the total number of civilian workers to just over one hundred by May 1865.

With the death of General Totten in April 1864, the newly appointed chief of the corps of engineers, General Richard Delifield, construction of Fort Clinch halted. The new chief of the corps was in the process of reevaluating the forts of the third system and seeing what could be done to improve them so that they could continue their service in defending the nation. Advancements in artillery production occurred during the war, and the Army Corps of Engineers needed to examine it. General Delifield requested the engineer officers to provide recommendations to the third-system forts for their continued service. Major General John G. Foster responded to this request, and his report was studied so much so that Delifield asked that further information be forward to him. The recommendation was as follows:

1. Increase the thickness of the curtain walls by filling in the Shendo do Rhonde and sealing up the rifle ports along the curtain walls.

Left: Major Alfred F. Sears served from 1862 to 1865 as the commander of the fort and chief engineer in charge of construction. *Author's collection.*

Right: To extend the service of Fort Clinch and other third-system forts, Major General John G. Foster called for modifications. *Courtesy of the Library of Congress.*

2. *Reduce the height of the two barracks and storehouse buildings along with the bastion tops.*
3. *Remove the sand hills to the southwest of the fort.*
4. *Build new bombproof quarters and support building.*
5. *Have only one access ramp to the top of the fort, allowing for more bombproof structures.*
6. *Install the new large-caliber rifle cannons within the fort and construct a new battery position just outside of the fort to the east.*

These recommendations and modification would allow for the continued use of Fort Clinch to defend the area's waterways.

The following were United States Army Engineer Officers that directed the construction of Fort Clinch from 1847 to 1867.

Major George Dutton, 1847 to 1852
Captain James L. Mason, 1850 to 1853
Captain Jeremy F. Gilmer, 1850 to 1857

Captain William H.C. Whiting, 1857 to 1861
Captain Arthur H. Dutton, April 1862 to July 1862
Captain John W. Barlow, 1865 to 1869

The following were the fort's assistant engineers.

Second Lieutenant George W.C. Lee, 1854 to 1856
Second Lieutenant William Merrill, 1859 to 1861

The following officers directed construction from 1862 to 1865 and were officers in the First Regiment New York Volunteer Engineers; they served in Company E, which was assigned to Fernandina and Fort Clinch from 1862 to 1865.

Captain Alfred F. Sears, chief engineer, 1862 to 1865; Promoted to Major
*   January 1865*
First Lieutenant Hiram Farrand, assistant engineer, 1862 to 1864
Edward N.K. Tallcott, assistant engineer, 1862 to 1864
Second Lieutenant Alexander F. Newman, assistant engineer, 1862 to 1864
John S. Allenson, assistant engineer, 1862 to 1864

The following are federal army engineers and infantry companies, battalions and regiments that served at Fort Clinch from March 1862 to May 1865.

First New York Volunteer Engineers Companies C and E (Company E,
*   1862–65, a detail after June 1864; Company C, 1862–63)*
Fourth New Hampshire Infantry (March 1862 to September 1862)
Ninth Maine Infantry (March 1862 to January 1863)
Seventh Connecticut Infantry (January 1863 to May 1863)
Seventh New Hampshire Infantry (May 1863 to June 1863)
Eleventh Maine Infantry (June 1863 to October 1863)
Ninety-Seventh Pennsylvania Infantry (March 1862 to April 1862, and
*   October 1863 to April 1864)*
157th New York Infantry (April 1864 to June 1864)
107th Ohio Infantry (June 1864 to September 1864, with two companies
*   remaining until December 1864)*
First South Carolina, later redesignated the Thirty-Third USCT (January
*   1863 to February 1863)*

Third USCT (March 1864 to May 1864)
Fourth USCT (July 1863 to December 1863)
Eighth USCT (June 1864 to July 1864)
Twenty-First USCT (May 1864 to September 1864)
Thirty-Fourth USCT (August 1864 to January 1866)
Seventh United States Infantry (1865 to 1869)

Other companies and battalions also served at Fort Clinch with very limited service time, including the Third Connecticut, Seventh USCT, Third New Hampshire, Second Florida Cavalry and Third Rhode Island Heavy Artillery.

Arriving in May 1865, the Seventh United States Infantry of the regular army took up the post–Civil War occupation of Fort Clinch and the towns of Fernandina. Ordnance sergeant Charles Wendell also arrived in May and was assigned as the first ordnance sergeant stationed at Fort Clinch; he oversaw the care and maintenance of the fort's artillery and buildings. In 1867, four new cannon platforms were finished, and four fifteen-inch Rodman Columbiads were installed. The massive cannon weighed fifty thousand pounds and could fire solid shots that weighed four hundred pounds with exploding shells that weighed three hundred pounds up to four thousand yards. In addition to the fifteen-inch cannons, there were also eight twenty-four-pound howitzers mounted in the bastions, and two field guns were also in service: a ten-pound Parrott rifle and a twenty-four-pound field howitzer. The remaining artillery was dismounted and removed to the fort parade field. At the batteries around Amelia Island, the army was charged with dismantling and moving the artillery to the Fort Clinch Pier in 1866 and 1867. The Old and New Town batteries, along with the railroad bridge battery, were removed, and some sixteen cannons and thousands of rounds of ammunition were relocated to the Port of Fernandina and to Fort Clinch.

From 1869 until the reoccupation of Fort Clinch during the Spanish-American War, three army ordnance sergeants oversaw the care and upkeep of the fort and its artillery. The following ordnance sergeants served at Fort Clinch from 1865 to 1900.

Charles Wendell, 1865–79
John Barr, 1878–88
William Liuder, 1898–1900

In 1864, new cannon platforms were installed to mount fifteen-inch Rodman Columbiads, the largest to ever be installed in the fort. *Courtesy of the State Archives of Florida.*

From 1888 to 1898, the fort was secured, and agents from the U.S. Quarantine Station that were located on the Fort Clinch Military Reservation maintained the fort's security. Military inspections were held annually by officers of the corps of engineers and ordnance corps from Savannah, Georgia.

4
UNITED STATES COLORED TROOPS

D uring the war, the army actively recruited men of color. Although men of color served in the War for American Independence and the War of 1812, the organization of African American regiments of infantry, troops of cavalry and batteries of artillery for the federal army was truly birthed during Civil War; the United States Navy, on the other hand, had allowed free men of color to serve long before the Civil War. During the war, Gideon Wells, the secretary of the navy, allowed escaped slaves to serve in the navy, and in truth, the navy was the first branch of the military to be integrated. Although the organization of African American men into soldiers was conducted with little to no approval from the commander in chief and the War Department, it did occur in the early part of the war.

The First South Carolina Volunteers got their start on May 7, 1862, when under Special Order No. 84 was issued by the headquarters of the Department of the South. The order directed Sergeant Charles Trowbridge of Company F, First Regiment New York Engineers, to assemble a small group of ex-slaves to be organized and trained in military drills. Other attempts to organize African American soldiers were taking place in Kansas with the First Kansas Volunteers, and in Louisiana, under the command of General Benjamin Butler, the Native Guards, or Corps Afrique, were being assembled.

An issue soon arose as to what to do with persons of color when the federal government was at war, and many wondered whether the people of color who were under the custody of the federal army were considered free. In the case of General John Frémont, he declared martial law in Missouri and stated that all slaves were free. President Abraham Lincoln had strong opinions on the institution of slavery, and he personally and politically hoped to see it end. The president, not wishing to see the border states join the Confederacy or discontinue their support of the Union, was forced to counter the order given by Frémont.

On August 6, 1861, President Lincoln signed into law the Confiscation Act, which allowed the United States government to confiscate any and all property that was being used by the South to support the Confederate military or its rebellion for Southern independence. That property also included slaves. At the time, slave labor was being used to construct fortifications and other defenses; they were also working in the production of military equipment and arms manufacturing, and they were tending crops that were used to feed the Southern population and the Confederate armies. For the South, it was making use of a labor force that, by law, was legal and needed given the manpower shortages due to the war.

Prior to the recruitment of men of color by the federal army, slaves were, in many cases, considered captured spoils of war (contraband), especially under the Confiscation Act. The relationship of African American soldiers to Fernandina and Fort Clinch needs to be examined. The African American soldiers of the First South Carolina Volunteers were the first African American soldiers to serve on Amelia Island. Although their time on the island was extremely short, the role they played in the military operations in the area helped advance the opportunity to create additional African American units, especially along the South Carolina, Georgia and Florida coasts.

By the fall of 1862, the First South Carolina was a regiment of former slaves ready for military service with the approval of the army and the secretary of war, Edwin Stanton. In November, Thomas Wentworth Higginson was appointed colonel of the regiment. Higginson was already serving in the federal army as a captain in the Fifty-First Massachusetts Infantry when he was offered the command of the First South Carolina. He served as colonel until his health forced him to resign in October 1864. A minister

In January 1863, the First South Carolina Volunteers, the first colored troops at Fort Clinch, arrived. *Courtesy of the State Archives of Florida.*

and well-known abolitionist, Higginson led a battalion of the First South Carolina in January 1863 on its first military mission as a new African American regiment in federal service to Florida.

After arriving at Fort Clinch and Fernandina by ship, most of the troops did not disembark; those who did were on display, and the conduct they observed was that of surprise and excitement from the white troops of Fort Clinch and the Post of Fernandina. The concerns over how these new soldiers were going to perform and whether they could serve at all were shared by many who observed them. For the African American population living in Fernandina at the time, it was moving for former slaves to observe this new regiment of African American soldiers; the regiment gave them hope for the future of the African American race in America. If a former slave could become an American soldier, surely a race of people could be free.

The mission of the First South Carolina answered the question of whether African American men were able to fight, and it proved that free black people and former slaves were willing, if need be, to die for liberty and freedom. During the month of January 1863, the First South Carolina saw action up and down the Saint Marys River in Florida and Georgia. They also engaged the Confederate Home Guard forces in what was called the Battle of the Hundred Pines; they inflicted causalities on the Confederate forces but not without causalities of their own. The First South Carolina suffered the loss of two men and seven wounded. They also captured a large store of lumber and livestock, along with nearly forty thousand bricks for the continued construction of Fort Clinch.

Following the First South Carolina's military operations, reports carried the news of their success in trial by combat. The Emancipation Proclamation of January 1, 1863, further allowed for the recruitment of African American troops, both free and formerly enslaved. Just five months later, the Bureau of Colored Troops was established when General Order No. 143 was issued on May 22, 1863, by the War Department. The order classified African American soldiers as United States Colored Troops or (USCT). By the end of the Civil War, there were 119 infantry regiments, 11 regiments of heavy artillery, 6 cavalry regiments and 10 batteries of light artillery. African American soldiers served in just about every campaign, with the exception of just a few. From 1863 to 1865, the total number of enlisted African American soldiers, according to the United States Army, was 186,097. Of those men, 29,038 died in service; however, the adjutant general furnished a report to the army's surgeon general on October 25, 1870, that said the number of African American troops that died in service was 33,380, along with 285 white officers who died in command of African American troops. That report brought the total number of dead to 33,665 officers and enlisted men. For going above and beyond the call of duty, sixteen African American soldiers were awarded the nation's highest award: the Medal of Honor. It was a true testament to the troops' dedication, duty and service.

Following the service of the First South Carolina in January 1863, the next African American troops to serve on Amelia Island belonged to the Fourth Regiment Colored Infantry. Organized at Fortress Monroe in 1863, three companies made up the battalion that served at the Post of Fernandina, with some limited duty at Fort Clinch. The soldiers of the Fourth USCT were engaged in the construction of Fort Neglee, which was also referred to as Battery Neglee; it was under construction in Old Town Fernandina. After a short stay, two companies rejoined the regiment, and Company A remained there until December 1863. The Fourth USCT served in several capacities from securing the towns to manning the various picket posts; they also served as the guards for the post's headquarters, which were located in the home of former senator David Yulee. They also received regular instruction in heavy and light artillery drills at the battiers and at Fort Clinch.

To show their military capabilities and to help encourage former slaves to join the army, the Fourth USCT regularly held company drills on the streets of Fernandina for all to view. In June, a portion of the Eighth USCT conducted scouting operations and patrols in Nassau County, just west of Amelia Island. The regiment was organized at Camp William Penn in Philadelphia, Pennsylvania, in September 1863 and mustered in on December 4, 1863. The regiment was assigned to the Department of the South and was moved to Jacksonville, Florida, in February 1864. There, he served in the federal expeditionary forces led by Brigadier General Truman Seymore. After it was assigned to Colonel Hawley's Brigade, the Eighth USCT saw combat at the Battle of Olustee, Florida, on February 20, 1864. There, it suffered the loss of its commander, Colonel Charles Fribly, along with 310 casualties. Following the battle, the unit returned to Jacksonville and remained there with limited operations in Duval and Nassau County. Three companies spent a month in service at Fernandina, where they also received a course in artillery instruction. In August 1864, the regiment was transferred to Deep Bottom, Virginia.

The Third USCT saw service in Jacksonville, Florida, after arriving there in February 1864; it remained there until May 1865. One company and, later, two companies served at Fernandina, where the African American troops underwent heavy artillery instruction over the course about three

The U.S.C.T. were vital in military operations in Fernandina and at Fort Clinch from 1863 to 1865. *Courtesy of the Library of Congress.*

months at Fort Clinch. When not conducting artillery drill, soldiers of the USCT were provided soldiers to the provost marshal for picket duty around Amelia Island; afterward, which they rejoined the regiment in Jacksonville. The Third USCT was organized in Philadelphia, Pennsylvania, in August 1863, and it was mustered in later that year. The unit saw a great deal of military service and was involved with the Siege of Fort Wagner on Morris Island, South Carolina. It was also involved in operations against Charleston until January 1864. It was then that the unit moved to Hilton Head, South Carolina, and in February, it was transferred to Jacksonville, where it took part in expeditions from Jacksonville in May and June 1864 that were directed against the Confederates at Camp Milton.

With the end of the war in May 1865, the Third USCT was still in service and was about to be mustered out when a mutiny took place while the regiment was in Jacksonville. On October 29, 1865, a soldier of the Third was found guilty of stealing food—in this case, molasses—from the regiment's mess and was ordered to be punished by the officer of the day, Lieutenant Greybill. The punishment was to tie the soldier up by his thumbs, and it was to be done on the regiment's parade field, where all soldiers of the Third could witness the punishment. While the guilty soldier was on display, a group of soldiers stood together and demanded their comrade be cut down; they said if he was not cut down, they would do it themselves. As the soldiers approached, Lieutenant Greybill, who was then joined by Lieutenant Colonel Brower, the regiment's commander, drew his pistol and fired into the group of soldiers, hitting Private Joseph Green. This caused the soldiers to retreat, only to proceed to take up their rifles and return. In a few moments, this turned in to a pandemonium, with the exchange of shots and shouts to shoot the officers. More soldiers swelled the ranks of those leading the charge against the officers, while other soldiers, along with the noncommissioned officers, tried to subdue what had become a mutiny. The event was a total chaos, with one officer seeking assistance from another company that was posted nearby.

With the help of the NCOs and other soldiers, the event came to an end. However, the soldiers who were involved were placed under guard, and they had to fight to save their lives. Mutiny was a punishable offense, and if they were found guilty, they could be executed. Fifteen soldiers were put on trial and fourteen of them were charged with the violation of Article 22 of the articles of war. Of all the soldiers who took part in the mutiny, six soldiers were sentenced to be shot by firing squad, and the other soldiers were sentenced to prison. The six soldiers who were to be executed were transferred to Fort Clinch, where their sentences were carried out. On December 1, 1865, the six soldiers were executed just outside the west wall of Fort Clinch. The executed soldiers were Private Thomas Howard, David Craig, James Allen, Joseph Nathaniel, Joseph Green and Jacob Plowden. In the case of David Craig, it was possible that he was innocent of the mutiny; however, the attempt to prevent his execution came too late, and he was executed with the others. It seems that, in several cases, the treatment of African American was somewhat harsh, and in the case of the Third USCT, the white officers in command ruled with strict discipline. All of the federal troops, whether they were African American or white, were governed by the army regulations and the articles of war. Although white soldiers were executed during the conflict, the treatment and hardline discipline of the African American troops is a matter to ponder.

African American troops were supposed to be paid the same as white troops; however, this was not the case. Their pay was reduced on the grounds that they were African American soldiers. And sometimes, the equipment and weapons they were provided with were inadequate or just unfit for soldiers to have in the first place. But whatever the obstacle, African American soldiers performed their duties and hoped to be seen as equals in the eyes of the government and people they were defending. Their service in the army was the steppingstone to the freedom they sought.

Throughout the summer of 1864, several military expeditions were conducted from Fernandina using only African American troops, and in July, a portion of the Third and Eighth USCT conducted a raid on Callahan,

Florida, just west of Amelia Island. In late July, they were also involved in the engagement at Brandy Branch. To continue the recruitment of African American men for the army, the Fourth Regiment South Carolina Infantry of African Descent was organized in Fernandina in July 1863. After its organization, the men received military training, forming the raw recruits into soldiers. In addition to the instruction in infantry training, the men also received artillery instruction, which was conducted at Fort Clinch. The Fourth Regiment South Carolina was consolidated with the Third South Carolina after it was assigned to the Post of Fernandina until January 1864, and it thereby became the Twenty-First USCT. In March 1864, in order to continue recruitment after the regiment left, a detachment remained behind in Fernandina under the command of Captain M.E. Davis until the summer of 1864. In 1864, the colored troops finally received equal pay, which caused great rejoicing among the ranks of colored troops, as many had refused to accept the reduced pay that was initially offered to them.

In August 1864, another raid was conducted along a length of the Florida Railroad by the 34th, 35th and 102nd USCT, along with the white troops of the 75th Ohio Mounted Infantry. The raid was meant to keep pressure on the

From December 1864 to May 1865, the Thirty-Fourth United States Colored Troops were the only infantry troops serving at Fernandina. *Courtesy of the Library of Congress.*

Confederate Home Guard forces and civilians, and it was meant to disrupt the line of supplies being provided to the southern army. In December 1864, three companies of the 34th USCT were posted in Fernandina and at Fort Clinch, and they served as the only federal infantry forces on Amelia Island from December 1864 to May 1865. The regiment was assigned to several posts in Florida during the war. The 34th was the last of the African American units to serve at Fort Clinch and in Fernandina until the Spanish American War in 1898.

From 1863 to 1865, African American troops served in Fernandina and at Fort Clinch as companies or battalions. The following African American units served there.

First South Carolina, later redesignated the Thirty-Third USCT
Third USCT
Fourth USCT
Eighth USCT
Twenty-First USCT
Thirty-Fourth USCT

In addition, the 7th, 35th and 102nd USCT were assigned to Fernandina for an extremely short period of time and only as a detachment or company. African American soldiers played a significate role in helping bring an end to the Civil War. Both free African Americans who were already living in the northern states and former slaves from the southern and border states answered the call to defend and preserve the Union. These men made up the regiments of USCT, and today, we should honor and remember their sacrifices and service to the nation.

The Thirteenth Amendment, which was eventually passed, abolished slavery. After the issue of slavery was settled in the United States, the next battle was the struggle for equality in the post–Civil War era. The war demonstrated that African American men were able to perform the duties of an American soldier. After the Civil War, the United States Army maintained African American units that served in the Plains Indian Wars and other later conflicts. African American soldiers have come a long way since the days of the Civil War, and today, they are examples of the best that America has to offer.

5

RECONSTRUCTION AND
CIVIL WAR VETERANS

E ven before the war ended in 1865, the former citizens of Fernandina
began returning to Amelia Island. These former residents were
unhappy with the conduct of the Civil War and the living conditions
they endured. Upon returning home, they were required to give an account
of themselves to the federal authorities and were obligated to take an oath of
allegiance to the United States. As soon as the island was secured by federal
forces in March 1862, northerners began arriving, and many conducted
business with the army and navy.

With the end of the war, many of the prewar residents returned to
Fernandina after leaving with the Confederate forces in March 1862; they
looked to return to the lives they once had. The returning citizens had to
deal with a large number of northerners who had moved into their towns
during the war and who wished to remain after the war was over. Many
former slaves also called Fernandina home, as they had gone to Amelia
Island seeking freedom and the protection of federal forces; after the war
was over, they wanted to start a new life. Federal soldiers who served at
Fernandina during the war were also looking for a new start, and many of
their families moved to the island. It is this postwar growth that was a driving
force of Fernandina and Amelia Island during the Reconstruction era.

With the death of President Abraham Lincoln, Vice President Andrew
Johnson ascended to the office of president of the United States. Johnson
inherited the unfinished business of healing the nation, along with the
reconstruction of the South. Unlike Lincoln, whose leadership and political

Captain John P. Martin commanded Company B of the Seventh United States Infantry, serving at Fernandina and Fort Clinch. *Courtesy of the Library of Congress.*

resolve was a driving force during the conflict, Johnson needed to rise to the needs of the nation. Greatly influenced by the cabinet and the strong politicians of the House and Senate, Johnson's administration moved forward to create a new life for the citizens of the South through Reconstruction.

In Florida, Johnson appointed William Marvin, a pro-Union Southerner, as the acting governor. Johnson's administration believed Governor Marvin would greatly help the state in the postwar reconstruction, as he appealed to southerners, northerners and former slaves. He called for a constitutional convention, which convened in October 1865 and was the first of several conventions to assemble. It repealed the Ordinances of Secession of 1861 and the ratification of the Thirteenth Amendment for the abolishment of slavery. Marvin was tasked with many challenging issues, ranging from reestablishing state and county governments and trying to prevent, if possible, the former state leaders from regaining the offices they had held before and during the Civil War. Although slavery had come to a legal end, black codes were used to keep African Americans as second-class citizens. To curtail these efforts, the United States Congress continued carrying out the work of the Bureau of Refuges, Freedmen and Abandoned Lands, which was a great help to the African American community in Fernandina and throughout the South. The army became a major player in the reconstruction of Florida and elsewhere in the South, and it was tasked many issues that the army was not accustomed to handling. The army carried out the work of civil government.

The army maintained its occupation of Fernandina, and new troops continued to arrive during Reconstruction. Three companies of the Seventh United States Infantry arrived on May 27, 1865, and they were assigned to Fernandina. The Seventh served as the primary law enforcement unit until civil authority was reinstated to ensure that the laws of the country were applied and obeyed. Still serving at Fernandina and Fort Clinch were three companies of the Thirty-Fourth USCT, and they remained there until January 1866, along with a small detachment of soldiers from the First New York Volunteer Engineers, who were preparing to muster out and leave by the of end of June 1865. Under the command of Major Alonzo A. Cole, the new post commander of Fernandina, the Seventh U.S. Infantry was directed to post troops in the same locations as the Thirty-Fourth USCT. The Seventh assigned troops to both towns and a company to the fort. The combined forces of the Seventh and Thirty-Fourth USCT totaled 351 officers and men. The troops were about to be inundated with returning civilians, former slaves and northerners.

Fernandina's first order of business was to reinstate its government's functions, including elections. As early as April 1865, Fernandina was in the process of electing its town leaders, with 160 African American votes and 9 white votes, the citizens elected Adolphus Mot as mayor, along with five aldermen. Since it was the first postwar election to take place in Florida, the chief justice of the United States, Salmon P. Chase, administered the oath of office to Mot and the other elected members while on a tour of the Florida. Mot's time as mayor was short; a new election was held, with Samuel T. Riddell elected as mayor, along with six new aldermen. In addition to the city's government, the court system was reestablished to enforce the state and local laws that were needed to operate the community.

The war also brought with it the famed carpetbaggers who were looking to profit on anything of value. With many unpaid taxes due to the war, the opportunity was ripe for the picking in this seaside community. The Florida Railroad laid in disrepair on the mainland, and its owner, David L. Yulee, was imprisoned at Fort Pulaski in nearby Savannah, Georgia. The port harbor pilots had directed navy ships during the war and were prepared to handle an increase in civilian merchant ships that were looking to deliver goods, coal and water in their vessels. The return of the U.S. Customs Service added greatly to the operations of the Port of Fernandina. The relighting of the lighthouse and the installment of new ship channel markers added to the growth of the seaport and the towns. The telegraph line was reinstalled to send and receive information that greatly helped the community and sped up the delivery of news and orders to the military forces stationed on the island.

The returning citizens were faced with the possibility that their prewar homes were unavailable, as they had either been sold for unpaid taxes or were in use by agents in the U.S. government. Many homes were also occupied

The post–Civil War era in Fernandina was a time of growth for the area's towns and seaport. *Courtesy of the State Archives of Florida.*

by army and navy personnel or were simply purchased by Northerners who had arrived on the island during the war or before the former residents had returned. In the case of former Confederate general Joseph Finegan, his home was sold and turned into an orphanage and school for African American children, and former U.S. senator Yulee's home was still in use by the army as a headquarters. Still, many homes were unoccupied, which allowed some former owners to once again take up residency; that is, if they were able to pay the taxes that were due. With the return of the court system came the prosecution of citizens who were being held by the federal military for civil crimes, and the army turned the citizens over to the reestablished civil authority. The towns were truly returning to normal, and the future was starting to look bright for their citizens.

At the time, a large group of Confederate veterans called Fernandina home. Many of them had lived there before the war, and others were seeking something new. They were working together to grow the community in peaceful times, even if that meant working with former enemies. The former Confederates who resided in Fernandina and Amelia Island included William Naylor Thompson, a former corporal of the Seventh Regiment Florida Infantry who served as an elder of the Presbyterian Church, a railroad paymaster and a state senator in the postwar era. They also included James F. Tucker, who served in the militia forces and went on to serve with the Second and Ninth Florida Infantry; he was also a ship captain and Fernandina's harbor master. Henry Linville, a former captain in the Confederate army, was a postwar naval inspector for the Port of Fernandina. Alonzo B. Noyes served as a captain in the militia forces at the beginning of the war and raised a local company of militia, known as the Coast Guard Artillery, to defend the island, and he owned several businesses in Fernandina. William H. Garland, a sergeant in the Eighth Florida Infantry and, later, a Nassau County revenue assessor, was another former Confederate in Fernandina. Captain Augustus O. MacDonell served with the First Florida Infantry and went on to work as a railroad agent in postwar Fernandina. Other former Confederates who also called Fernandina home were:

Charles C. Mann, Tenth Kentucky, postwar blacksmith and machinist
Martin L. Merson, Third Florida Infantry
Orrick B. Murry, Second and Eleventh Florida Infantry, postwar carpenter
Daniel Weimer, Second South Carolina Infantry
James Sims, Third South Carolina Infantry

Warren F. Scott, Fifth Florida Infantry, postwar collector of revenue and
   a printer
Jackson Mizell, Twenty-Sixth Georgia Infantry, postwar timber agent
Henry J. Muller, Forty-Seventh Georgia Infantry
Robert Harrison, Major Quartermaster, C.S. Army
Ephraim Harrison, Second Florida Infantry
Samuel Boyd, Fourth Georgia Cavalry
William Cushing Mathews, Georgia Artillery
Charles Allen, Forty-Fourth Georgia and Cobbs Legion,
George Arnett, Second Georgia Cavalry and Twenty-Fifth Georgia Infantry

Lieutenant Edward J.K. Johnston served in the Confederate navy and was a citizen of Fernandina before the war. While serving in the Confederate navy, he was taken prisoner and died as a prisoner of war. In October 2002, his remains were returned to Fernandina and laid to rest beside his wife in the Bosque Bello Cemetery. It was a humble honor for a brave citizen of Fernandina to be reunited with his loved ones, if only in death.

Mary Martha Reid was one of the most notable female citizens of Fernandina to serve with the Confederate forces. The wife of former territorial governor Raymond Reid, she traveled to Richmond, where she, along with Dr. T.M. Palmer, opened the Hospital for Floridians. There, she served as the matron. After already losing her husband and one son to yellow fever, she lost her remaining son, Raymond Jenkins Reid, fighting for the cause of Southern independence in the Battle of the Wilderness in May 1864. Mary's sister Rebecca was married to Confederate general Joseph Finegan. After the end of the war, Mary returned to Fernandina and was very active in the community.

Georgia Fairbanks arrived in Fernandina by invitation of Senator David Yulee in years before the Civil War; there, he worked as a clerk for the Northern District of Florida. He assisted the U.S. government in acquiring the property for Fort Clinch in 1842, and he also served as a territorial senator, the first president of the Florida Historic Society and an editor of the *Florida Mirror* newspaper. During the Civil War, Fairbanks served in the Confederate Army of the Tennessee as a quartermaster officer with the rank of major. After the war, he resided with his family in Fernandina and was a vital part of the postwar growth of Amelia Island. Following the end of the war, General Joseph Finegan attempted to acquire his home in Fernandina but was unsuccessful and later moved to Jacksonville, Florida.

The Civil War veterans of Fernandina rest in the cemeteries of Amelia Island and Nassau County. *Courtesy of the State Archives of Florida.*

With the release of David Yulee from prison, he went to work repairing the Florida Railroad, and he eventually sold it. Yulee eventually left Fernandina and moved to Washington, D.C., but not before regaining his fortune from the railroad he built before the war.

Many federal soldiers who served at Fort Clinch and elsewhere witnessed the horrors of war, and the peace of Fernandina was a welcome sight after four years of conflict. Like their former Confederate enemies, they sought a new start on Amelia Island.

Major Ferdinand C. Suhrer served at both Fernandina and Fort Clinch with the 107th Ohio Infantry Regiment. After the war, he operated a boardinghouse in New Town. In 1884, Suhrer was killed in a dispute with another resident. Major Suhrer, Captain Fredrick E. Grossman and Lieutenant Colonel Mark Downie served in the Army of Potomac, and all three fought at the Battle of Gettysburg in July 1863. At a postwar Remembrance Day event that was held in New Fernandina, the men shared their account of the battle, and subsequently met monthly with other veterans to socialize and recount the war. Lieutenant Colonel Downie worked in the newspaper business, and Captain Grossman was a U.S. customs agent.

Fredrick E. Grossman immigrated to the United States and joined the U.S. Army in 1855. By the beginning of the Civil War, he was the sergeant major of the Seventh U.S. Infantry. After the regiment was paroled in Texas, it joined the Army of the Potomac in 1862; in 1864, the regiment was sent to New York City to assist in putting down the draft riots. When he arrived with the regiment in Florida after the war, Grossman was a first lieutenant; he was stationed at Fort Clinch until 1869. Afterward, Grossman was transferred to the Seventeenth U.S. Infantry, and in 1875, he resigned from the army and returned to Fernandina as a customs agent under former major William Duryee. It was during one of the worst yellow fever epidemics that Captain Grossman died on September 29, 1877. On a special note, during the Seventh Infantry's occupation of Fernandina, First Lieutenant Grossman was tasked with the recovery of the remains of federal soldiers who were killed at Battle of Olustee on February 20, 1864, near Lake City, Florida. In 1866, he, along with a detachment of the Seventh, gathered the remains of over one hundred federal soldiers for burial.

Federal army veteran Major William B.C. Duryee served as the acting assistant adjutant general of U.S. volunteers and was wounded at the Battle of Antietam in September 1862. He later became the deputy collector of customs for Fernandina's port and a pillar of the community in the postwar era. Samuel T. Riddell had served in the Seventh New Hampshire and became the mayor of Fernandina and, later, the postmaster. Major Thomas Leddy was wounded in the war while serving with the famed Irish Brigade in the Sixty-Ninth New York Infantry. He served the last year of the war as provost marshal for the Post of Fernandina, and he became the proprietor of the Florida House Inn. Captain Robert S. Schulyer served with the Thirteenth New York Cavalry before he was wounded in 1864. He was later the architect and designer of the postwar Saint Peters Episcopal Church and several homes throughout the town.

The following men served in the federal army or navy and later became citizens of Fernandina.

William Houghton, Tenth Pennsylvania Infantry
Joseph Burkhardt, Seventh Illinois Infantry
Romeo Denegall, Federal Navy, USS Perry
Samuel King, Federal Navy
Jamain Roswell, Federal Navy

A portion of the Twenty-First United States Colored Troops were recruited at Fernandina, and many African American men called Fernandina home before joining the federal army. The following men, along with others from the regiment, returned to Fernandina: James Eubanks, Benjamin Hatchie, Plato King, Charles Knabb, E.F. Langley, Simon Nathan, Pablo Rogers, Richard Thomas, Little Washington, James Williams, Stephen Wright, David Moddy and Michael Panton.

Veterans of the First South Carolina later redesigned the Thirty-Third USCT, which also called Amelia Island and its towns home. The First South Carolina was one of the first all–African American regiments that were recruited and was completely made up of former slaves. These men served along the Saint Marys River in January 1863 and spent a very short time at Fernandina in January and February 1863. After the war, these men became Fernandina citizens: Benjamin Wright, Amos Atkinson, Peter Morris, Glascow Taylor, James Edwards, Joseph Hunter, Hampton Jones, James King and Peter Miller.

James William served in the 34th USCT, William Johnson and Jefferson Harris served in the 35th USCT and Isaac Platt was a veteran of the 104th USCT. All of them were residents of Fernandina and held various jobs in the community, including jobs with the railroad, the timber businesses and the Port of Fernandina; they were carpenters, craftsmen, farmers

In 1869, Fort Clinch was placed in caretaker status, where it remained until its next call to service. *Courtesy of the collection of Dicky Ferry.*

and office holders in the city's and county's government. Three of them became officers of the law, and the others became church leaders and inn keepers. No matter their jobs in the postwar era, the one thing that bound them together was their service in the federal army in defense of the Union.

The timber boom was the greatest postwar growth in Fernandina. With virgin forests of oak, pine and cypress trees and the Port of Fernandina, the towns were brought into their golden eras. By 1868, Reconstruction was coming to an end, and the South was beginning to recover from the war. The towns' populations were growing, and with new schools, churches, homes and businesses on the rise, the port was becoming busier each day, with more ships arriving to pick up vast amounts of lumber. On June 18, 1869, the Seventh United States Infantry left Fort Clinch. The fort was placed into caretaker status; the first ordnance sergeant, Charles Wendell, oversaw the care and protection of the fort until 1878, when John Barr took over until 1888. Both ordnance sergeants served in the army during the Civil War, and in addition to overseeing the fort's care, they were both involved in community affairs; ordnance sergeant John Barr even became the mayor of Fernandina in 1888.

To provide for the veterans of the Civil War, two societies were established: the Grand Army of the Republic and the United Confederate Veterans. These organizations allowed the veterans to come together, socialize and promote the history that they played a part in during those years of struggle. The veterans regularly attended yearly memorial observances to remember their comrades who gave their lives during the Civil War, fighting for the Union or Confederacy. The veterans, along with the other citizens of Fernandina, truly made Fernandina alive again after four years of war, and they were the driving forces in the community that we enjoy and live in today.

NOTES

Chapter 1

1. Letter to the mayor of Charleston, South Carolina, from Joseph Finegan, militia commander of the Fernandina Volunteers, 1860, the State Archives of Florida.
2. Quote from the letter of Thomas H. Broome, from the collections of Mary and Bob White.
3. Quote from the letter of Felix Livingston, from the collections of Mary and Bob White.
4. Letter to General Joseph G. Totten from Captain Daniel P. Woodbury, in *The War of Rebellion, Compilation of the Official Records of the Union and Confederate Armies*, Series 1, vol. 1.
5. Quote from the letter of Felix Livingston, from the collections of Mary and Bob White.
6. Quote from the letter of Benjamin Thompson, from *Civil War Times Illustrated Magazine* 1973.
7. Letter from Colonel W.S. Dilworth to the Confederate government, in *The War of Rebellion, Compilation of the Official Records of the Union and Confederate Armies*, Series 1, vol. 1.
8. Response to Colonel W.S. Dilworth from the Confederate government, in *The War of Rebellion, Compilation of the Official Records of the Union and Confederate Armies*, Series 1, vol. 1.
9. F.L. Dancy letter to Governor John Milton of Florida, in *The War of Rebellion, Compilation of the Official Records of the Union and Confederate Armies*, Series 1, vol. 6.

10. Quote from the letter of T.H. Broome, from the collections of Mary and Bob White.
11. Quote from the letter of William Hagan, from the collections of Mary and Bob White.
12. Quote from the letter of William Hagan, from the collections of Mary and Bob White.
13. Letter to General James H. Trapier from Confederate general Robert E. Lee, in *The War of Rebellion, Compilation of the Official Records of the Union and Confederate Armies*, Series 1, vol. 6.

Chapter 2

14. July 5, 1861 report, in *The War of Rebellion, Official Records of the Union and Confederate Armies*, Series 1, vol. 53.
15. Quote from the letter of Captain Goodrich, from the collections of Lewis G. Schmidt.
16. Report of the Ninth Maine Attack by Lieutenant Colonel H. Bisbee, in *The War of Rebellion, Compilation of Official Records of the Union and Confederate Armies*, Series 1, vol. 6.
17. Quote from the letter of Edward Miller, from the author's collections.
18. Quote from letter of Frances Norman, from the author's collections.
19. Quote from letter of Levi Rury, from the collections of Patrick Lands.
20. Quote from letter of Charles Culver, from the collection of Patrick Land.
21. Letter to the handling of prisoners assigned to Fort Clinch, from the National Archives, record group 92.
22. Quote from letter of Charles Culver, from the collection of Patrick Land.
23. Quote from letter of Henry Harrington, from the author's collections
24. Letter to the post provost marshal from the post surgeon, from the National Archives, record group 92.
25. Provost marshal notice to organize a town militia, from the National Archives, record group 92.

Chapter 3

26. Quote from the letter of George D. Hughes, from the collections of William "Bill" Bulger.

BIBLIOGRAPHY

Anonymous. *Historical Register and Dictionary of the Army*. Vols. 1 and 2. Washington, D.C.: Government Printing Office, 1903.

Davies, William Watson. *The Civil War and Reconstruction in Florida*. New York: Columbia University Press, 1913.

Dyers, Frederick H. *A Compendium of the War of the Rebellion*. Vol. 1. New York: Thomas Yoseloff, 1959.

Gibson, Charles Dana, and E. Kay Gibson. *The Army's Navy Series*. Vol. 1, *Assault and Logistics, Union Army Coastal and River Operations, 1861–1866*. Camdon, MA: Ensign Press, 1995.

Hartman, David W., et al. *Biographical Roster of Florida's Confederate and Union Soldiers, 1861–1865*. 6 vols. Wilmington, NC: Broadfoot Publishing Company, 1995.

Hillhouse, Don. *Heavy Artillery & Light Infantry*. Jacksonville, FL: Don Hillhouse, 1992.

Higginson, Thomas Wentworth. *Army Life in a Black Regiment*. Boston: Fields, Osgood and Co., 1870.

Johns, John E. *Florida During the Civil War*. Gainesville: University of Florida Press, 1963.

Lewis, Emanuel Raymond. *Seacoast Fortifications of the Unite States*. Novato, CA: Presidio, 1979.

Long, E.B., with Barbara Long. *The Civil War Day by Day: An Almanac, 1861–1865*. New York: Da Capo Press, 1971.

Official Records of the Union and Confederate Navies in the War of the Rebellion, thirty volumes. Washington, D.C.: Government Printing Office, 1894–1927.

Patrick, Rembert W. *Aristocrat in Uniform: General Duncan L. Clinch*. Gainesville: University of Florida Press, 1963.

Phisterer, Frederick. *Statistical Record, A Treasury of Information about the U.S. Civil War*. New York: John Kallmann Publishers, 1996. Originally published in New York in 1883 by Captain Frederick Phisterer.

Pollard, E.A. *The Lost Cause: A New Southern History of the War of the Confederates*. New York: E.B. Treat & Company, 1867.

Proctor, Samuel. *Florida a Hundred Years Ago*. Gainesville: Florida Civil War Centennial Commission, 1960–65.

Quarles, Benjamin. *The Negro in the Civil War*. New York: Da Capo Press, 1989.

Roberts, Robert B. *Encyclopedia of Historic Forts*. New York: Macmillan, 1988.

Robertson, Fred L. *Soldiers of Florida in the Seminole, Indian, Civil, and Spanish-American Wars*. Live Oak, FL: Democrat Book & Job Print Company, 1903.

Schmidt, Lewis G. *The Civil War in Florida*. Vols. 1 and 2, parts 1 and 2, *Florida's East Coast*. Allentown, PA: Lewis G. Schmidt, 1991.

The War of Rebellion: Compilation of the Official Records of the Union and Confederate Armies. Washington, D.C.: Government Printing Office, 1880–1901.

Weaver, John R. *A Legacy in Brick and Stone: American Coastal Defense Forts of the Third System, 1816–1867*. Missoula, MT: Pictorial Histories Publishing Company, 2001.

Welcher, Frank J. *The Union Army, 1861–1865: Organization and Operations*. Vol. 1, *The Eastern Theater*. Bloomington: Indiana University Press, 1989.

ABOUT THE AUTHOR

Frank A. Ofeldt III started his career as a volunteer with the Florida Park Service in the late 1980s as a historical interpreter in the Fort Clinch Living History Program. After college, he accepted a position with the agency and was assigned to Fort Taylor State Historic site at Key West, Florida; he was later transferred to Fort Clinch State Park, where he currently serves as park service specialist, having served twenty-seven years with the agency. He is the author of two books that were published through Arcadia Publishing and The History Press. He continues to serve the community of Fernandina Beach as a local historian on military history of the island; he was also the president of the Duncan Lamont Clinch Historical Society and a former board member of the Amelia Island Museum of History. Today, he is a member of the American Historical Association, the Society for Military History and the Council on America's Military Past. He is an avid reader, lecturer and collector of American military antiques.